Discovering America

Victor Nuovo

Burlington, Vermont

Copyright © 2022 by Victor Nuovo

All rights reserved. No part of this publication may be reproduced, distributed, or transmitted in any form or by any means, including photocopying, recording, or other electronic or mechanical methods, without the prior written permission of the publisher, except in the case of brief quotations embodied in critical reviews and certain other noncommercial uses permitted by copyright law.

Onion River Press
191 Bank Street
Burlington, VT 05401

Publisher's Cataloging-in-Publication data
Names: Nuovo, Victor, 1931-, author.
Title: Discovering America / by Victor Nuovo.
Description: Burlington, Vt: Onion River Press, 2022.
Identifiers: LCCN: 2022901058 | ISBN: 978-1-957184-01-2
Subjects: LCSH United States--History. | Political parties--United States--History. | Political science--United States. | Political science--United States--History. | United States--Politics and government. | BISAC HISTORY / Americas (North, Central, South, West Indies) | HISTORY / Essays | HISTORY / United States / General | POLITICAL SCIENCE / History & Theory | PHILOSOPHY / History & Surveys / Modern | PHILOSOPHY / Political | PHILOSOPHY / General
Classification: LCC JA84.U5 .N86 2022 | DDC 320/.01/1--dc23

Acknowledgement

I owe an enormous debt of gratitude to friends and benefactors without whose encouragement and assistance these essays would never have been written or published: Paul Ralston, Angelo Lynn, John McCright, and to Sue Hoxie, who prepared the volume for the printer, and to Betty, my wife and dearest friend, "the angel glow that lights a star".

Contents

BEGINNINGS	1
Light At The End Of The Tunnel	3
Discovering America	7
The Anger of Bartolomé de las Casas	12
The Worldview of Sir Walter Raleigh	17
Errand into the Wilderness	22
The Mind of New England Puritanism	27
The Carolina Colonies	32
The Consequences of Slavery	37
FOUNDING	43
The Very Idea of a Democracy	44
Independence	49
The Case for Independence	54
More on Independence	59
Questioning Common Sense	64
John Adams on Government	69
The First American Confederacy	73
Constitutionalism	79
Federalism	84
Anti-Federalism	89
Founding Brothers	94
Founding Sisters	99

I

ESTABLISHMENT	105
Mercy Otis Warren's America	106
Thomas Jefferson	111
George Washington	115
Benjamin Franklin	121
Adams and Jefferson in Retrospect	126
Growing A Divided Nation	131
The Political Thought of John C. Calhoun	136
The Age of Jackson	141
Establishing the Rule of Law	146
TRANSCENDENTALISM	153
Transcendentalism	154
A Platonic Digression	159
Margaret Fuller	163
Ralph Waldo Emerson	167
Emerson on Experience	172
Thoreau at Walden Pond	176
Civil Disobedience	180
Walt Whitman	185
IMPERIALISM	191
Manifest Destiny	192
The Trail of Tears	196
The U.S.-Mexican War	201

Civil War	207
The American Civil War	208
Was the Civil War Inevitable?	213
A Nation "Concieved in Sin"	217
William Lloyd Garrison	222
Frederick Douglass, The Experience of Slavery	227
A House Divided	232
The Politics of Emancipation	237
Gettysburg and Beyond	242
Reconstruction	247
Reflections on the Civil War	252
Expansion and Social Reform	257
Reflections on the Frontier	258
How the West Was Won	263
American Imperialism	268
Remembering the Ladies	273
The Mind of Elizabeth Cady Stanton	278
Theodore Roosevelt's Progressivism	283
Racism and Science	288

War and Peace	293
Woodrow Wilson	294
The Great War	298
Herbert Hoover and the Great Depression	303
FDR and the New Deal	307
FDR and the Second World War	312
Elusive Peace	316
Franklin Roosevelt's Women	320
The Indomitable Frances Perkins	325
Where Do We Go From Here?	331
The New Frontier	332
What Does It All Mean?	336

VICTOR NUOVO

BEGINNINGS

DISCOVERING AMERICA

Light At The End of The Tunnel

Human beings are social animals. Like ants, bees, wolves, lions, elephants, gorillas and chimpanzees, they live in communities. But, we humans differ from other social animals in a very distinctive way. Other animals depend on the members of their hive, pack or herd, gathered over generations in one hospitable territory, to sustain them.

Humans depend upon these things as well, but, perhaps because we possess an infinite sense of space and time, we are an expansive, perhaps an invasive species, whose habitat knows no limit and who imagine we are players in history. For that reason, we depend upon traditions. A tradition is a form of life that is handed down by one generation to the next. It is taught, learned, practiced, revised, enlarged and often reformed. It is always renewable as long as those who use it have the will and the courage to keep going.

A language is a tradition. It is one of the first things we learn in childhood. Our parents teach us, and soon the members of our community become our teachers. We go to school and learn to read and write — and also to count, which depends upon another indispensable tradition of signs, namely, numbers. We practice our language every day in ways that are beyond counting. We would be lost without it. We would lose our means to communicate, not only with others, but also with generations still to come; our consciousness would become a life denying wasteland, a meditation on death. Language is the tradition on which all other human traditions depend and by means of which they flourish and perpetuate themselves.

Try to imagine what politics would be like without language. It would be nothing. And this is most likely true of much else that we do, even of something as sensual and intimate as making love. But my concern is with politics, for as human life has evolved, politics has emerged as the all-encompassing frame in which all the other activities of human life take place. It is essential to today's life.

And as Thomas Hobbes has said, without well-founded political institutions, human life would exist in a chronic state of war; life would become "solitary, poor, nasty, brutish and short." Whatever misgiving, suspicion, foreboding, or despair we may feel towards the present state of politics, the alternative of an apolitical life would cause us even more distress. Some individuals may prefer to escape, to withdraw from politics, seeking comfort and consolation in the company of their family and friends; others may merely seek to be alone with themselves, to lead a solitary meditative life. But if this is an escape, then it is cowardice, and, in the end, it provides still greater opportunity for political predators to have their way and wreak even more havoc than they do now.

Yet there is no doubt that a pall has settled upon our life together these past few years, especially on our political life; a deep gloom of despair encircles and entwines us.

Nationally, our political institutions have become stained with corruption, neutered by incompetence, and stupefied by ignorance. Some of the media is little better. The desperate voices of self-promotion of Fox News and elsewhere fill the air with their nauseating slogans, accompanied by music that is equally loathsome and foul. Even our institutions of learning have joined the chorus, these training-grounds for future politicians and entrepreneurs have forgotten the love of learning and search for truth; once temples of truth, they have refashioned themselves for success in their ceaseless campaigns for capital advancement and in the competition for students.

In response to these doleful activities, the jeremiad may be the only fitting form of literary expression today — mournful, gloomy and sorrowful. And in the face of all this, living where we do in this lovely town, surrounded by natural beauty, comforted by birdsong, with caring friends close by, and having the freedom to move about as we choose and associate with whomever brings us cheer and enjoyment, we are tempted to let the greater world pass by unnoticed and unregarded, while we hide our heads in the sand.

Or we can gird up our loins and arm ourselves with wisdom and understanding and confront our current disorder and reasons for discontent, and, so outfitted, take on the world.

Now, the best weaponry available to us for this task is knowledge, knowledge of our political traditions, of its ideas and practices, laws and institutions, and the historical events that engendered them. This is my purpose: to present in a series of essays about the American political tradition, not as a curiosity, but as a weapon, to combat corruption, and as a healing balm, a weapon-salve to heal our ills and to bring comfort to our souls, and as a shield, the shield of justice.

By the American political tradition, I mean the political ideas and practices of the United States of America. There are two ways of approaching this tradition. Narrowly, by studying its founding documents, in particular, the Declaration of Independence, the Constitution and Bill of Rights, and later, the Emancipation Proclamation. The study would be of their origin, use and influence.

Another approach is by broadly considering the founding of America and the political circumstances that led to it and followed from it, and also the older traditions of political thought, including the opinions of the great personages who informed it. And from these beginnings, to trace the development of American political life down to the present. I shall travel this broader and longer path.

I am grateful to the *Addison Independent's* publisher, Angelo Lynn, for giving me the opportunity to present these essays in my hometown newspaper over the past several years.

And it is altogether appropriate that he should include political essays of this sort and political commentary as part of his weekly offerings. I am reminded of Sinclair Lewis's 1935 novel, "It Can't Happen Here," a fictitious tale of the United States falling prey to fascism. The hero of the story is the editor of just such a newspaper in a Vermont town much like Middlebury, a man who had the courage of his convictions. The story is still pertinent, and also poignant; reading it is a source of courage.

Besides, the small-town newspaper is also a tradition, noble and inspiring, an indispensable edifying instrument of American democracy. Long may it prosper! Our freedom depends upon it.

Discovering America

ALL OF US ONCE LEARNED IN SCHOOL that Christopher Columbus discovered America on October 12, 1492. But now we all know this is not true. Columbus was not the first person, nor even the first European to discover

America. Norsemen beat him to it by approximately half a millennium.

But millennia before the Norsemen, other peoples crossed over from Asia, by land or sea, to America and settled here, so that what Columbus discovered, when he discovered America, was not just land, but people, and not just people, but mankind, which is to say, he discovered the diversity of our species, a truth that every generation must learn anew. Here, I follow David Abulafia, a historian at the University of Cambridge, who has written a wonderfully readable and informative book about Columbus' discoveries, which he has aptly entitled, "The Discovery of Mankind."

The land, of course, was not yet called America, and the people whom Columbus first encountered were not uncivilized savages as has been mistakenly supposed. They were Arawaks — the name refers to a linguistic family, and to a people now virtually extinct, but whose customs and language, and, more generally, whose culture has survived.

The people made a favorable impression on Columbus. He described them in his logbook: "They were well built with fine bodies and handsome faces," "they have very straight legs and no bellies, but well-formed bodies." He noted their hair was coarse "like that of a horse's tail," which they wear short, except long at the back.

They painted themselves, but wore no clothes. Their bodies bore wound scars, indicating that they had engaged in warfare to defend their settlements, yet they carried no weapons. They were friendly and eager to trade and gave the Europeans what seemed the best of the bargain, most fatefully, pieces of gold, to which many Europeans had become addicted, for European greed would be their undoing.

Yet, Columbus did not regard them as equals. He imagined rather that the natives would make good servants for he observed "that they soon repeat anything that is said to them" and he went on to remark "that they would easily be made Christians for they appeared to me to have no religion."

He kidnapped a half dozen of them, samples to take back to Spain to display to Ferdinand and Isabella, the Spanish monarchs who funded his voyage. He supposed that in this way, they would learn the language and be more useful in this new subservient role.

There is no doubt that Columbus thought that these natives were human and worthy of being converted to Christianity, also possessed of intelligence and an immortal soul. Thus, by converting them to Christianity, he believed that he was providing for their happiness in another world to come after death. But in this world. at least, they were to his mind only part of the riches of America, the bounty claimed by him and by the many European adventurers who followed him. Perhaps a level above merchandise.

In "The Discovery of Mankind," David Abulafia tells about the discussion at home that was caused by Columbus' discoveries, and the many that followed. Who were these people? Were they all descendants of Adam, or did God create mankind more than once? And if so, were these different versions of mankind equal. And if they were truly human, how was it that they had no religion, and that only now, 1,500 years after Christ they were to receive the advantage of conversion to Christianity?

And since most of those who reflected on these questions believed in God and divine providence, they wondered what God's purpose was in this long delay in bringing them salvation?

But there was no doubt that they made good servants, for they were teachable. Unfortunately, nature didn't cooperate with these plans. The adventurers who followed Columbus in search of wealth and cheap labor enslaved the natives and put them to work under the harshest conditions in gold mines. What followed was "massive mortality," genocide, not deliberate perhaps, but the effect of cruel bondage, for the Europeans needed workers "to extract gold, and later sugar."

The labor shortage that followed led to "the massive importation of black African labor," which was the beginning of American slavery, which would continue for three and one-half centuries.

Columbus was an adventurer. In this respect, he was typical of his age: the Renaissance. The leading personages of this age regarded themselves as discoverers, not only of new lands, where they might find gold and other commodities to enrich them, but also of forgotten knowledge, that was buried in the past in Greek and Roman literature.

Two centuries would pass before the European horizon expanded to include the universe. The way was opened by Copernicus, Tycho Brahe, Johannes Kepler, and decisively by Galileo, who had the advantage of the telescope. But the path to this vast panorama of nature was already prepared.

In 1417, Poggio Bracciolini, a Renaissance scholar in search of forgotten classics, discovered a copy of Lucretius's "De rerum natura" [On the nature of things] in a monastic library in Italy. In his work, Lucretius depicted an infinite universe containing worlds without number, coming to be and passing away, all under the direction of an indifferent nature, whose only principles were chance and necessity, diversions of matter at play. The first printed edition of "De rerum natura" was produced in 1473, nearly two decades before Columbus discovery of America.

But to return to America, it is curious that this new continent was not named Columbia. Perhaps this was because Columbus did not suppose he had discovered a new continent. Nor did Amerigo Vespucci, a Florentine, a cartographer and ethnographer; he was more interested in the land and the peoples than in gold.

In 1508, he was appointed chief navigator of Spain. After several voyages, he concluded that South America was, if not a continent, a great landmass, separate from Europe, Asia and Africa. A noted German cartographer, Martin Waldseemüller, fashioned a world map, and named this landmass America, after its presumed discoverer. There are other derivations of the name. One of them, a Mayan name *Ammerique,* signifying a group of mountains in Nicaragua. Another attributed the name to Richard Ameryk, a wealthy Englishman who underwrote the voyages of John Cabot.

The Anger of Bartolomé de las Casas

WHEN COLUMBUS FIRST LANDED on the island of Hispaniola on October 12, 1492, he claimed the land for the Spanish monarchs, Ferdinand and Isabella, and he give it its name, which means "Spanish Island". Columbus claimed all the riches of the land, including not just its material goods, but also its native people. Whereas the land remained the possession of the Spanish monarchs, grants were made to their European subjects to work the land and for this purpose they were granted also the free use of the native people as workers or forced labor. The European settlers were called encomenderos; the grants they received were called encomienda, literally, things held in trust. But the practice was slavery in every way but in name.

Bartolomé de las Casas (1484–1576) took part in the Spanish conquest of Cuba in 1502, and he became an encomendero; but he became troubled by his livelihood, for although it brought him physical comfort and modest wealth, he was increasingly horrified by the cruelty of its methods and the suffering that it caused.

On December 12, 1511, Las Casas heard a sermon preached by the Dominican monk, Antonio Montesinos, in the Church of Santo Domingo. He was deeply moved by it, especially by these challenging words:

> "Tell me by what right of justice do you [encomenderos] hold these Indians in such a cruel and horrible servitude? By what authority have you waged such detestable wars against these people who dwelt quietly and peacefully in their own lands? Wars in which you have destroyed such an infinite number of them by homicides and slaughters never heard of before. Are these not men? Do they not have rational souls? Are you not obliged to love them as yourselves? Why do you keep them so oppressed and exhausted, without giving them enough to eat or curing them of their illnesses which they incur from the excessive labor with

> which you burden them; they die, or rather
> you kill them, in order to extract and
> acquire gold every day?"

According to one historical account, the realization began to grow in Las Casas' mind that one could not be a Christian and also practice slavery, for all Christians are enjoined to love their neighbors as themselves, and every human being is one's neighbor, and one must treat them as equals. But full realization took three years. It should be noted that Las Casas had become a priest, and shortly before he heard the fateful sermon, he had himself become a Dominican monk. The Dominican order was dedicated to preaching, to the conversion of infidels and heretics by persuasion. Three years after hearing Montesinos' sermon, while preparing to preach one himself, Las Casas, read this text from Ecclesiasticus 34:21–2:

> The bread of the needy is their life: He that
> defraudeth him thereof is a man of blood.
> He that taketh away his neighbor's living
> slayeth him; and he that defraudeth the
> laborer of his hire is a bloodletter.

These words reminded him of Montesinos' sermon. He spent days agonizing over them and he emerged from his agony with this triumphal conviction: "that everything that had been done to the Indians in the Indies [that is, in the so-called new world colonies] by European colonists was unjust and tyrannical." And it became his sole purpose in life thereafter plead the Indian cause before the Spanish monarchs and their court. He became a self-appointed lobbyist for the Indians. He also wrote many historical works, telling the sad story of European colonization, which included a multi-volume "History of the Indies", as also "A Short Account of the Destruction of the Indies".

Perhaps most noteworthy about these works, is that they not only tell a tale of European cruelty and destruction, but Las Casas takes time to describe just what was destroyed. The so-called Indians were not transient wanderers, they had settled the land and established civil societies and created a civilization. He observes that on the one island of Hispaniola there were five Indian kingdoms. And he notes that the rulers of these Kingdoms quite willingly accepted the sovereignty of Spain and sought its protection. But the colonists preferred a practice of conquest, or rapine, rape, slaughter, and enslavement. Thus, they destroyed not only persons, but peoples, and civilizations. It was genocide on a grand scale.

"A Short Account" is not an easy book to read. One's mind is beset by anger, a madness that cannot be assuaged by justice, for justice would come too late, and it would be a mere matter of words.

Yet it is justice that Las Casas desired, and his efforts were not without some result, albeit of little enduring effect. He returned to Spain many times to plead the cause of the Indian before the Spanish court. And it would seem that the Spanish monarchs, who considered themselves upholders of Christian morality, were at least troubled in conscience. The Queen, Isabella declared that Indians were not to be enslaved, that they were her free subjects. And there were efforts at legal reform. The institution of encomienda was abolished. Instead, prospective Conquistadors were enjoined that before attempting to make a conquest of land, they were to read a declaration or rather an ultimatum, requiring the hearers to acknowledge their subjectivity to the Spanish Crown, to the Pope, and to the "One True God". This was often done peremptorily and often out of hearing of the Indians and was followed swiftly by pillage and destruction. Las Casas, when asked what he thought of this measure, responded that he didn't know whether to laugh or cry.

Las Casas was also the inspiration of the so-called Black Legend. The term referred largely to propaganda that circulated during the seventeenth and eighteenth centuries by Dutch and English Protestants, and later, depicting Spanish cruelty as unmatched as it were beyond the pale. Excessively cruel it was, but it was not unmatched. One need only consider the story of how the West was really won.

Postscript: Las Casas' *A Short Account of the Destruction of the Indies,* has been translated into English and published by Penguin. The editor, Anthony Pagden, has written an illuminating introduction. It should be required reading in all our schools. Also, David Abulafia's *The Discovery of Mankind*, mentioned in the previous essay is a readable account of the richness of the civilizations that were destroyed.

The Worldview of Sir Walter Raleigh

THERE IS A WELL-ESTABLISHED TRADITION among political philosophers that there are three types of government, distinguished according to the number of persons who rule: one, few, or many; hence, monarchy, oligarchy (or aristocracy, when the few are of noble character), or democracy. For the sake of consistency, the latter might have been designated "demarchy," but this word has another meaning. A demarchy is a form of representative government of a city or state, which is subdivided into districts. The people of each district choose their representative or "demarche," either randomly or by preferential vote. The demarchs make up a council with the power to govern. In a pure democracy, there is majority rule of all the people in a common assembly. Accordingly, a demarchy is a representative democracy, a form of government with which we are intimately familiar: a democratic republic, that is, a representative government whose representatives are democratically selected, by popular vote.

In the wake of Columbus, the various European governments engaged in the colonization of America were monarchies, and the adventurers whom they empowered were all dedicated monarchists. During this age of discovery, the Pope, thinking himself to be the spiritual monarch of the world, divided this new world between the two leading Catholic political monarchies, Spain and Portugal. Little was known then of North America. Like Columbus, the Spanish Conquistadores claimed the lands of South and Central America for the Spanish monarchs, Ferdinand and Isabella, and for their successors. All this was accomplished by conquest.

The early English colonies in America were more interested in enrichment than conquest; they assumed that America was a wilderness, land free for the taking and for commerce. However, their politics were no different. The first English settlement in North America was established on Roanoke Island, in the Chesapeake Bay in 1585, and abandoned, settled again in 1587, and soon the whole area came to be known in the minds of the settlers as "The New-Found

Land of Virginia," named in honor of the English queen, which suggests that in spite of prior Indian settlements, and the commercial relations between them and the English, it was taken to be English territory, a domain of the Queen. Sir Walter Raleigh was a major sponsor and financier of the Roanoke colony. He was favorite of the Queen, who knighted him for his services. He was a Renaissance man: adventurer, statesman, soldier, entrepreneur, but also a poet, philosopher, scientist, and historian.

The Roanoke colony was ill-fated. The second settlement was also abandoned, how and by what cause, is unknown. Its settlers simply disappeared. According to one theory, they were massacred by the Indians, according to another, they were at the point of starvation and sought refuge with neighboring Indian tribes and were assimilated by them.

The first permanent English settlement was established in Jamestown ten years later. It was named after James I, who succeeded Elizabeth. Raleigh took no part in this later settlement. Indeed, when Jamestown was founded, he was a prisoner in the Tower of London. A few months after Elizabeth's death, he was accused of treason, of plotting against the James's succession. He was convicted and imprisoned for thirteen years. In 1616 he was pardoned and allowed by the King to lead an expedition in search of El Dorado, the legendary city of gold, supposed to be located somewhere in what is now Venezuela. His voyage enraged he Spanish, who considered this their territory. The Spanish ambassador persuaded James to punish Raleigh. The sentence of death was renewed, and he was beheaded on October 29, 1618. It was reported that when he mounted the scaffold, he asked to see the axe that would be used to kill him, and noting that its blade was very sharp, commented "This is a sharp Medicine, but it is a Physician for all diseases and miseries." His last words, to the executioner, were "Strike, man, strike!"

While in prison, Raleigh passed the time reading, writing, and reflecting. He was well supplied with all that he needed, books, pen, ink, and paper, and he wrote *The History of the World*. It is a masterpiece. It is also a very long work, and few have read the whole of it — I have not. But there is an abridgment of it that gives the sense of the whole. And it contains the reflections of a man of refined literary taste and penetrating thoughtfulness. It presents a view of the world, and of history, exemplary of its time, a succession of kingdoms and sovereigns, good, bad, and indifferent. Raleigh's preface gives a brief survey of English monarchy, it is frank and unvarnished. Reading it, one is reminded of Shakespeare's histories, which were written about the same time. They complement each other.

In his prison cell, Raleigh reflected on the meaning of history. It was a fitting subject to think about for someone in prison and under a sentence of death. It was a way of escape, for he perceived that history "triumphs over time" and its misfortunes. By studying history, we are no longer confined to the present moment. Historical memory and imagination transport us to the most distant times past, to the origin of the world, and to its successive generations. In the historical imagination the dead are made to rise "out of the depth and darkness of the earth" and pass in review in the present. Raleigh's purpose was not to escape his present misfortunes, but to judge them and himself, and to make even more universal judgments, to draw out of the past "a policy no less wise and eternal." Policy or policies of prudent social action, of just institutions and practices, of political wisdom, and there is a good deal of this, spread throughout the many pages of Raleigh's history. One can randomly open the book and read and be edified.

We are all prisoners of the present, and in these doleful political times, the present may seem a place of hopeless confinement. But, joining Raleigh to Aristotle, we are also historical and political animals; our greatest talents are historical memory and a capacity for prudent action; and history is our best teacher.

Postscript: Raleigh's cell in the tower of London was not a dark dungeon, nor was it anything like a modern jail cell. It was a spacious room, with windows, a fire place, cabinets, a writing desk and chair. It was large enough to accommodate a library of 500 books and also scientific equipment, for among other subjects that interested him was natural philosophy, especially chemistry, which allowed him to conduct experiments. Like all early chemists, Raleigh had was curious about the possibility of transmuting base metals into gold. A useful abridgment of Raleigh's *History of the World* was published in 1971 by Macmillan Press, edited by C. A. Patrides. It has a fine introduction.

Errand Into the Wilderness

"ERRAND INTO THE WILDERNESS" is the title of the book by the late Perry Miller, a distinguished historian of New England. Miller took it from the title of a sermon given in 1670. It was a common practice in colonial New England for the people of a town and their public officials to gather in church on election day to renew their commitment to God and good government. The sermon was billed as an election day sermon. The Puritan minister who gave it asked his congregation this question: "What purpose had sent them on this errand in the wilderness?"

The Puritans were English Protestants, proponents of the Reformation. Now the Reformation was both a religious and a political movement. According to its name, its purpose was to reform the Christian Church. Religious reformers desired to purify the church by restoring its authoritative constitution, beliefs, and practices, which they supposed were prescribed in the Bible. They believed that the Bible, and the Bible only, is the true word of God, where God chose to reveal his will for mankind; all Christians were obliged to study it and obey it and to regard it as their supreme authority in all matters of life and death.

However, some Kings of Protestant nations also saw in this an opportunity to increase their power. Hitherto, religious authority centered in the Church of Rome, whose bishop, the Pope, claimed that supreme and universal spiritual power resided in his office. But the Pope was also a temporal ruler and often used this power to interfere with affairs of nations.

In England, Henry VIII, seized the opportunity and in 1534 declared himself the supreme head of the Church of England and decreed that it be reformed. The architect of religious reformation was Thomas Cranmer, Archbishop of Canterbury, and among the notable products of his endeavor was The Book of Common Prayer and the Thirty-nine Articles. The former has become an English classic. But Cranmer's reforms did not satisfy the desires of many religious reformers. It kept too many of the institutions and practices of the Roman Church, and it maintained centralized authority in the Church, which now had two heads, one secular, the monarch, and the other religious, the episcopal hierarchy. This gave rise in England to the Separatist Movement, to the formation of independent churches, some of which prescribed the rule of a council of elders and clergy, Presbyterians, and others, local congregations often led by charismatic ministers who preached the plain Word of God. These were called Independents or Congregationalists. They adopted a form of government whose secular counterpart is still current in New England towns.

The oldest English settlement in New England was established by one of these congregations. They sailed from the Netherlands, where they first sought refuge--for they were religious refugees, and they reached Cape Cod on Nov. 11, 1620. This was not their intended destination. They had planned to establish themselves in Virginia. But fortune brought them to a different place, to a wilderness, that is, a place where there was no European political authority. Therefore, it became necessary for them to reinvent themselves politically just as they had already done religiously. And, while still aboard ship off Cape Cod, they drafted and signed the Mayflower Compact. It declares that the signatories had covenanted together, or mutually agreed, to combine themselves "into a Civil Body Politic." It stated their purposes, to glorify God, to promote the Christian faith, and to honor their King and Country, and also their intentions: "to enact, constitute and frame such just and equal Laws, Acts, Constitutions and Offices, as shall be thought most meet and convenient for the general good of the Colony." The compact was dated 11 November, anno domini 1620 [the date is according to the older Julian

Calendar; according to the Gregorian calendar, now in use, it was 21 November]; there were forty-one signatures, all men. There were others aboard ship who were not asked to sign: these included servants, and "merchant adventurers", and all the women. The congregation and their leaders believed it necessary to enact the political compact before they landed, because they feared that some among them, adventurers, would seize the opportunity of embarking in a wilderness, a lawless land, to engage in criminal behavior with impunity. The document is known as the Mayflower Compact.

The Massachusetts Bay Company began settlements in New England in 1630. The settlers did not regard themselves as refugees. The Puritans who settled the Massachusetts Bay Colony did not leave England to escape persecution, rather they left because they believed themselves God-sent to establish a new society in a new land, which would become a model to the world. According to one of their founders, John Winthrop, they were to become "a city upon a hill"; "a model of Christian charity"; an example to the nations; the eyes of all people would be upon them. This sense of mission, of American exceptionalism had its beginning and continues today, even though the religious context in which it was originally framed has lost its cogency to many. Yet the moral context is not lost. Winthrop was aware that there was great risk in exposing a civil society to the world. For, just as it could bring praise and reputation, it could also bring blame and ill-repute. A nation can also become a mockery, a symbol of wrong, a poster child of hypocrisy, an easy target for obloquy and verbal abuse. It is not clear what sort of model this country best represents to the world, especially now. If this were made a topic for debate, I am not sure which side would win the argument. It would be more profitable to set the debate aside and return to the study of this nation's history and its political tradition.

But before I leave this topic, I should consider the unhappy consequence of social modeling: persons or nations that imagine themselves to be models for others expect admiration and praise, or at least they hope for it; and when it doesn't come, when they find themselves rather held in contempt, ridiculed, and mocked, they become resentful, morose, sometimes vengeful. The chance that this will happen is highly probable, given the way the world is, filled with envy, ill will, selfishness, and self-pity. Indeed, it has happened, and we are living in with its consequences today. Exceptionalism is a risky business.

VICTOR NUOVO

The Mind of New England Puritanism

COTTON MATHER (1663-1728) WAS REGARDED in his time as one of the most learned persons in America. Born in Boston, educated at Harvard College, he became minister of a prominent church in Boston. He was a prolific author, publishing over 400 books. He is credited with bringing the thought of the European Enlightenment to colonial America.

He studied the works of Robert Boyle and Isaac Newton, with whom he corresponded, and was well versed in the new science, to which he made modest contributions in his careful descriptions of American flora and fauna and experiments in plant hybridization. He was also an early advocate of inoculation against smallpox, and was elected a fellow of the Royal Society of London. He was, of course, well grounded in theology and the Bible. He exemplified the flowering of the New England mind in all its scope and paradox.

It is paradox that I shall take as my theme. As an advocate of the new experimental science, Mather was convinced that the operations of nature proceeded according to physical causes that could be discovered through observation and experimentation. He was, in this respect, an empirical naturalist.

But he also believed in divine providence; that is, he believed that all events in nature and human history are pre-determined by the will of God. Nothing happens by chance. And because he believed that God is the moral governor of the world, he supposed that all events are divine communications, that there is some divine meaning in them which we should try to ascertain.

On the other hand, as an experimental scientist, albeit an amateur, he believed material nature operates according material causes in a lawlike manner, according to a law of nature discoverable by experimental research. But he also believed in spirits; indeed, he supposed that there was great invisible spiritual world surrounding the visible material one, just as the heavens surround the earth.

I should point out that this was not an unusual belief for the age in which Mather lived. His contemporary, the English philosopher John Locke believed the same. Locke believed that we form an idea of spirit by reflecting on the operations of our minds, which he supposed are not material but spiritual, although he confessed to have no idea what sort of thing a spirit is, and he conjectured approvingly from a human standpoint contemplating the great chain of being that there are probably a greater number of species of spirits above us than there are species of animals below us. He supposed that human life is unique because unlike other species it participates in spirit and matter (about whose nature, he also confessed ignorance except that it was tangible).

Yet, because he imagined that mankind is closer to the lowest of material beings than to God, the highest of spiritual beings, mankind does not stand midway in the chain of being, rather, closer to the bottom than the top.

His friend, Robert Boyle agreed, but this did not stop him from trying to communicate with "spirits of the air." Both Locke and Boyle claimed to be as certain of the existence of spirits as they were of material bodies. These views were commonplace among the 17th Century elite in England and in colonial America.

Mather became notorious because of his role as an apologist for the infamous New England witch trials, a role that he took upon himself with some misgiving, which he expresses in his book The Wonders of the Invisible World, where he gives an account of the trials and of many supposed instances of the spirit world.

Here is another paradox: Mather believed that God governs the world with an absolute power, that nothing opposes his will, which is purely good and unremittingly just. If malignant spirits operate in the world causing harm, it is because God has allowed it. God allows malicious spirits to cause harm as a means of punishing their victims or perhaps testing them.

I should add that Locke and Boyle, and their friend Isaac Newton, believed the same. They also believed, like Mather, that the world is in its last age, that human history will soon come to an end, and that a sign of this is the increase of the activity in the spirit in the physical world as it heads towards its consummation. One sure sign of this was an increase in evidence of spirit possession and witchcraft, and it was an infatuation with this idea that was the root of these malignant beliefs.

The witch trials were legal procedures against individuals who were accused of practicing witchcraft, of using spiritual power to cause mischief or harm. In 1691, Sir William Phips, a protégé of Mather's father, Increase Mather, became royal governor of New England. Cotton Mather wrote of the occasion in his great history of the colony: Magnalia Christi Americana. He writes that it was a time "when a governor would have had Occasion for all the Skill in Sorcery."

Especially among the young, there was an increase in the practice of magic, fortune telling, spells, and suchlike practices; people suffered from unexplained ailments, psychological and physical. "Preternatural Vexations upon their bodies, and a variety of cruel torments, which were evidently inflicted from the Demons, of the Invisible World"; deformations in the birth of animals and of humans. Among the torments were "spectres": phantoms or ghosts or intangible presences of persons well known to the tormented, intangible yet malevolent and terrifyingly threatening. There appeared to be an epidemic of such occurrences, a mass hysteria. And the cause of these disorders was thought to be men and women, mostly women, who had become possessed of the devil, who were known or suspected (and the suspicion was rarely if ever rational) of practicing witchcraft.

Now, Mather did not for a moment doubt these spiritual disorders, and he wrote about them with enthusiasm and in great detail. He believed that God allowed them, for although such circumstances "subvert government" and cause the ruin of civil society, God may sometimes allow them as a reminder to the people that it is only because of the restraint that he lays upon devils and infernal spirits that the world is not always so afflicted. This, of course, is a rationalization. But he also believed that trials must be subject to the rule of law, and to the law of evidence.

To his credit, in sermons and other public discourses, Mather counseled judges and warned them that they must not give unwarranted credit to witnesses of witchcraft. In particular, he questioned the credibility of witnesses who experienced torment from spectres, that is, spirits who were visible only to themselves. He considered them doubtful for there was no corroborating evidence, no witness of the cause of the victim's torment, and that without corroborating evidence a fair and rational judgment could not be made against the accused.

This curious mixture of the rational and the superstitious is a chief characteristic of the New England mind, perhaps even today. It was also characteristic of the mind of the early modern English elite, such as John Locke and Robert Boyle and Isaac Newton. And, allowing for cultural differences, it may be a characteristic that is still very much with us, chronic if not natural.

The Carolina Colonies

It is common belief that the English philosopher John Locke was one of the principal founders of modern liberalism. Central to liberal doctrine is the principle that all human beings are born free and equal, and that no human being has the right to rule another without his or her consent, and then, only in ways that do not infringe on the native right to liberty common to all. Locke's liberalism is a thesis professed by many notable scholars and even more by politicians; it has become a mantra, repeated in political speeches, but also in academic lectures and textbooks. However, it is at best a half-truth. And because Locke is commonly regarded as a precursor of American liberalism, it is important that a balanced and accurate picture of the man be carefully drawn.

You may ask, what has this to do with the Carolina Colonies? I will explain.

John Locke's status in English society was of the lower middle class. His father was a lawyer, who served as a court clerk. He was well connected, and through him, his son gained the sponsorship of notable men, and with their influence he gained admission to leading educational institutions: Westminster School—one of the leading English public schools—and the University of Oxford. At Oxford he studied the classics, mastered Greek and Latin, and gained a sufficient knowledge of Hebrew to allow him to become familiar with the latest biblical scholarship. After completing his undergraduate studies, he had to choose between one of the professions: law, medicine, or theology. He chose medicine and took a bachelor's degree in medicine. He later became a research assistant of the leading English physician, Thomas Sydenham, and together they did fundamental research in the transmission of infectious diseases.

Like many educated young men of modest means, it became necessary that Locke find a sponsor. He was fortunate in finding a position as family physician in the household of Anthony Ashley Cooper, a man of great wealth and political influence, who would soon become Lord Chancellor of England and ennobled, becoming the first Earl of Shaftesbury. As a member of Shaftesbury's household, Locke did much more than look after the health of Shaftesbury and his family. He was Shaftesbury's intellectual companion and secretary.

Shaftesbury became his political mentor. And he shared in his political fortunes. Among Shaftesbury's achievements was the founding of the first political party in England. Indeed, he may have invented the very idea. I will write more about parties in a future essay.

In 1670, the king, Charles II, appointed Shaftesbury one of eight Lords Proprietors of the newly established Carolina colonies. The Lords Proprietors constituted a grand council to conduct the business of the colonies. Locke was appointed its secretary. Among the council's first tasks was to draft a constitution. Shaftesbury most likely presided and is believed to be the principal author of what became known as "The Fundamental Constitutions of Carolina." Locke oversaw its several stages of revision and may also have composed parts of it.

Given the liberalism of Shaftesbury and Locke, one would expect that their liberal views would be reflected in the constitution. They were not. The form of government prescribed for the Carolina Colonies was not democratic, but feudal. Carolina was to be a county palatine. "County" is an English term signifying the chief administrative districts of England. A county palatine is an administrative district established by Royal authority and ruled by a hereditary lord or lords, who enjoyed a degree of autonomy. Two fifths of the land was divided between them, and they possessed the authority to subdivide their portions and grant them to lesser lords, who enjoyed a similar autonomy. Locke was made one of these lesser lords of manor and held the title of Landgraf; he later sold the property and gave up the title.

The Lords Proprietors and the lesser nobles did not themselves work the land, and few of them visited it. Rather they leased it to commoners who worked it. The remaining three-fifths of the land was divided into colonies, and it could be possessed by commoners, who farmed it. These are referred to in the "Constitutions" as freemen or freeholders, and altogether as "the people.

The colonies were governed by the Grand Council headed by the senior Lord Proprietor, and by a parliament, that met biennially. It was the principal legislative body and was constituted by all major and minor nobility — a House of Lords. The judiciary, and all the other administrative departments necessary to conduct civil business and maintain order and public safety also were under the direction of the lords. The land was leased to freemen, who cultivated it, and paid a yearly rent to the proprietors.

To qualify as a freeman, one must believe that God exists and "is to be publicly and solemnly worshipped" and must practice some religion. The policy was designed to encourage immigration by "heathens, Jews, and other dissenters from the purity of the Christian religion." The expectation was that this would put them in proximity to true Christianity, as practiced by the Church of England, and that after time reason and charity would persuade them to conform. Atheists were not included. This is hardly a liberal stance.

Finally, because agricultural labor was needed for the economy of the colony, slavery was introduced, and owning slaves became a right of all classes of society, including the lowest class of freemen. But slaves possessed no rights. Indeed, "every freeman of Carolina shall have the absolute authority over his negro slaves." Whether the scope of this authority included power over life and death is not stated, but it certainly meant that negro slaves were regarded not as persons, but as property. This is not liberal, indeed, it is as far from it as one can get.

The picture is different in Locke's "Second Treatise of Government." There it is prescribed that a civil society is formed by the consent of the governed, and that the people, who are all born free and equal, create their society by covenanting together. And Locke is emphatic, only the people, this collection of free and equal persons, is sovereign. This is the liberal Locke who was the guide to the founders of our nation. But even in this work, and in the new American nation, the people included only freeborn men. It did not include women. And it did not include "negro slaves." Yet it seems a contradiction to describe a civil society as liberal that allows the rights of freedom and equality only to a select class and gender. It is for this reason that I hesitate to characterize John Locke or his opinions as liberal.

The Consequence of Slavery

THE BEGINNINGS OF CONTACT between Africa and Europe occurred long ago, when the sea routes between the two continents were first opened. By the time Europeans began colonizing America, not only had commerce between all three continents been well established, but there were distinctive social and cultural evidences of their long association in the growth of mixed social groups, for the people not only traded, they cohabited, consensually or by force. Atlantic creoles were one of these mixed groups and their culture is a monument to this mixing; it is rich and vibrant; it took root in the Louisiana territory, and still flourishes there today, a venerable and artful part of American culture. This historical achievement is the starting point of a wise and informative history of the first two centuries of American slavery by Ira Berlin, entitled "Many Thousands Gone."

But Berlin's book is mainly about a sadder and ignoble heritage, American slavery.

The practice of slavery most likely began with civilization itself. As human societies enlarged and developed and cultivated the land and mined its depths, they produced commodities that required labor to produce them. As opportunities of enrichment increased through commerce, the need of laborers increased; and because the work was hard and toilsome and ill-suited to a gentile style of life, these laborers became themselves a disposable commodity that could be bought and sold. War, an inevitable consequence of commerce, provided a ready means of this commodity. Prisoners of war were believed to have forfeited their rights to life and liberty by having committed aggression against their captors. The Oxford English Dictionary defines a slave as an individual "who is the property of, and entirely subject to, another person, whether by capture, purchase, or birth; a servant completely divested of freedom and personal rights."

The United States of America began as a collection of *societies with slaves* that evolved into *slave societies*. This is an important distinction; it is central to the theme of American slavery. As I have observed, slavery is probably as old as civilization. But in America, like everything else that has happened here, it became big business. According to Ira Berlin, in a society with slaves, slaves play a marginal role in the economy of a society. Slaves were used to carry out household tasks, the most unpleasant ones, like cleaning latrines. In a slave society slavery is indispensable to the economy and not just to the household, and as I've already said, it had become big business. In his book, Berlin describes the process by which this happened. It began with the discovery that certain commodities: gold, silver, sugar, tobacco, later cotton, for which there is a market worldwide, and that great fortunes are to be made by producing them. Hence, the necessity to increase production.

And for this task, labor was needed. And because the work to secure these commodities is backbreaking, and not long endurable, a steady supply of labor must be found. Indians were on the scene, but their numbers quickly dwindled as a result of the genocidal practices of the colonists. Creoles were sometimes enslaved, but they were few. Importing slaves from Africa was the preferred solution. And, as, Berlin aptly sums it up, with all that, "slaveholders capitalized production and monopolized resources and consolidated their political power." The number of slaves increased dramatically; they "became the majority of the laboring class, sometimes the majority of the population." The great landowners enlarged their holdings, and as Berlin describes it, they "muscled other classes to the periphery," forced out small farmers, who, impoverished, marginalized, and disenfranchised, pulled up roots and headed west. The great plantations were not family farms, they were commercial enterprises ruthlessly managed. Their way of life of the has been famously romanticized, and sentimentalized by Margaret Mitchell in "Gone with the Wind":

> "There was a land of Cavaliers and Cotton Fields called the Old South. Here in this pretty world, Gallantry took its last bow. Here was the last ever to be seen of Knights and their Ladies Fair, of Master and of Slave. Look for it only in books, for it is no more than a dream remembered, a Civilization gone with the wind."

But beneath this shallow romantic facade was the cruel face of slavery. And here also lie the roots of racism, which is a recurring ailment that has infected the heart of America.

That the institution of slavery was a cause of American racism has been well-demonstrated by historians, and explained by social-psychologists, for it took root in the American conscience. It became easier to commodify other human beings if they were regarded as inferior, deemed not capable of a cultivated life or the enjoyment of the refined pleasures of civilization. And if slaves had features that distinguished them from the citizen population all the easier to set them apart. "Savages" and black Africans served this purpose better than uncultivated whites.

Not all Europeans who settled America were large landowners. The trend of the rich getting richer and the poor poorer continued, and among its effects was deep resentment among the smaller landholders, so-called yeomen farmers, resentful of their prosperous neighbors, whose proud demeanor and contumely added insult to injury. To compensate, they transferred their resentment to the victims of this prosperity, slaves, blaming them for their discontents, and regarded them as the cause of their incapacity to compete and their failure to grow rich.

The same motives led to hatred against Indians. Many small farmers, unable to compete with large landholders migrated westward towards the frontiers of the colonies only to find that the new lands they wanted had been reserved by treaty for Indians, who were also forced to move westward. They were outraged that the colonial government had granted territorial rights to the Indian nations, which made them forbidden to white settlers. Resentment for what was they took as gross injustice grew into hatred and often violence and popular uprisings; the story of how the west was won was not as heroic as it has been made out to be in the movies. American populism, fraught with moral ambiguity, had its roots here also. It is fair to conclude that the American character is a byproduct of slavery and territorial expansion.

One final thought. I often wonder why "Gone with the Wind" was so popular, as a book, a movie, and as a continuing legend. The book was published in 1936, the tail end of the Great Depression, and became a bestseller, a popular classic. The movie appeared in 1939, amid war and rumors of war. It too has become a popular classic and remains so today. Its popularity is a key to all the contradictions described above. There is something rotten in American Culture.

VICTOR NUOVO

FOUNDING

The Very Idea of a Democracy

EVERY CIVIL SOCIETY DIFFERS from every other one by virtue of its people, its language and culture, and its geography. Therefore, the question: "In what respect is this nation different from other nations?" is not idle. However, The United States of America is not only different from other nations, it is supposed to be exceptional. The question whether a civil society is exceptional is one of world-historical import. Those societies are exceptional that leave their mark on world history and civilization. It has become commonplace that proof of American exceptionalism resides in the fact that Democracy has, by default, come to be accepted worldwide as the paradigm or rule of government, whereas, before this nation's founding, in Europe, hereditary monarchy was the rule. Until the modern period, it was commonly supposed that hereditary monarchy was the original form of government, a natural offshoot of patriarchy, which was supposed to be the original form of the family.

Modern political orthodoxy no longer adheres to this opinion. Its paradigm is government by consent of the people, its origin a social contract, and it follows from this that the state does not belong to a ruling family, rather it is a public trust in which all the people share. And it is now commonly supposed that civil society originated in this way, and that democracy is its natural outgrowth. The self-creation of this nation, its rise, its growing power and influence, its world-historical success, is believed to have caused this change of mind. The change began slowly. The end of the First World War, which brought an end to European empires and the ascendency of the United States as a world power, is the point of no return.

To summarize, the universal acceptance of Democracy, rather than hereditary Monarchy or Aristocracy, as not only the standard of political correctness, but also as the form of government that is the most proper and the most durable, is viewed as a historical consequence of the historical achievement of The United States of America and the reason for its rise among the nations, its unmatched growth in wealth and power, and its worldwide influence, its seeming invincibility, which is taken as further proof that it will long endure. On account these things that America ranks high, perhaps highest, among the civilizations of world history. And this is the reason for her greatness.

But Democracy did not begin in America, rather it began in Greece, and it was because the founders of this nation were schooled in the Classics and enlightened by them that the American revolution has been described as "the result of reason," by which was meant, reason in a Greek idiom.

Tradition locates the origin of Democracy in Athens, where it achieved archetypal expression in the life and career of its great leader, Pericles (495–429 BCE). Pericles was an Athenian aristocrat, well-born, well-educated, and well-connected. He was no doubt highly intelligent, a patron of the arts, a lover of learning and of his native city, a true patriot, and brave. He was not much to look at physically — he had a bulbous head (hence, he is always depicted as wearing a helmet), and his frame was neither formidable nor graceful. But he was resolute and the force of his will made up for any physical deficiencies. He was popular among the people and was repeatedly elected to positions of political and military leadership. In these roles, he presided over the golden age of Athens. But this golden age was short lived.

Before the advent of democratic rule, the Athenian government was aristocratic. Certain families, through their wealth and ambition, rose to power until a single family seized power, and its head ruled as tyrant. [Tyrant, in Greek is closer in meaning to dictator than king.] He was overthrown in a popular uprising, and the people rose to power, and also came into possession of the city and its government. What gave power to the people was the large number of veterans of imperial wars. Athens had become an imperial power, a great sea power; the greatest in the Eastern Mediterranean, and by these means it increased its wealth and dominions. The sailors and marines, who enabled all this were not aristocrats but common men. When after service they returned to the city, they participated in elections and they were courted for their votes. Pericles, under whom many of them had served, and whom they greatly respected, became the first citizen of the city with their support, and under his leadership Athens became a nation "of the people, by the people, and for the people." He brought greatness to the city, not only politically and militarily, but by sponsoring the arts and architecture whose monuments, although now in ruin, still evoke wonder.

But the history of ancient Athens is a tragedy. Thucydides, also an Athenian, and a generation younger than Pericles, wrote an account of it in his *History of the Peloponnesian War.* The Peloponnese (literally, "Pelop's Island") is a great island west of the Greek mainland, connected to it by an isthmus. Its dominant city was Sparta, whose power rivaled Athens. They had become political rivals. These rivalries caused a great war between them, in which many other Greek cities became involved, supporting one or the other side. The war lasted a quarter of a century until Athens, its fleet destroyed, ignominiously blockaded and confined within its walls, was starved into surrender. Pericles died during the second year of the war, a victim of a plague that struck Athens.

Earlier in that year he was chosen by the people to deliver an oration on an occasion like our Memorial Day, honoring the war dead, those who had given their lives for the city. Thucydides gives an account of it. Pericles began by praising the ancestors from whom Athenians had received the city and the land, a free gift. This is just like the way we have received our town and its place. And the ancestors bequeathed a form of government along with it. It was not the rule of one person, or of a few, rich and privileged, but government of the many; whose leaders are elected from the people, by the people, and who rule for their good. Freedom of assembly and free expression, even in times of war, are a hallmark of the city, along with self-reliance in defense of the city. Vigilance not servility is the proper means of survival. And culture its heart and soul. "We cultivate beauty without extravagance, the love of wisdom without weakness, wealth not as a privilege or a means of self-aggrandizement or vain ambition, but as a means of action that benefits the city." The city is a school of virtue, a city on a hill, a heritage given to the world. The founders of this nation were cognizant of this idea; it was their model, and their aim was to establish a city whose glory would be a beacon to others, a light to enlighten. It is a noble idea, worth emulating. But it shines against the dark background of the tragic end of the golden age of Athens. It still shines.

Read Thucydides. He has many lessons to teach us.

Independence

WHAT HAPPENED IN PHILADELPHIA on July 4, 1776? On that day, or to be accurate, two days earlier, the delegates of 13 British colonies in North American, meeting in Philadelphia, declared their independence from Great Britain. The body of delegates that did this was the Continental Congress. It had been meeting on and off since 1774. It was created by the colonies to consider grievances against the colonial government of Great Britain and to seek redress for them from the British King and Parliament. The Continental Congress was not at first conceived as a government. However, the colonies had been at war with Britain since April 1775, and responsibility for waging it fell upon Congress. During the summer of 1776 it met to consider the question of separation of the colonies from Great Britain, and on the 2nd of July, it concluded its deliberations by declaring the colonies to be independent from the British crown, separate from Great Britain, yet of equal standing, that is, the colonies became 13 independent sovereign states. Two days later, on the 4th of July, "The Declaration of Independence" was adopted. It is the monument of the deed. But it is more than that, for the thoughts that it conveys were the very causes of the deed.

The British authorities regarded this deed an act of rebellion against lawful authority. The Congress disagreed. They regarded it as an altogether lawful act, sanctioned by nature and nature's God, by the law of nature discoverable by reason. They made this claim and offered proof of it in their Declaration. In this respect, the Declaration of Independence is a legal brief. But legal briefs are customarily presented to courts of justice, which have the authority to decide for or against them. In this case, there was no higher court to which the 13 colonies or the British government could appeal. There was only human reason, and on this account, The United States of America may properly be described as an original creation of reason. What was created? Thirteen independent states, united in their endeavor to remain free. But their action brought something else to be in the world: Independence itself, an idea, was let loose in history.

Having written these last few sentences, I find it necessary to pause and catch my breath, for they contain a very great thought. An entire philosophy of existence could be built upon it and in fact has been attempted many times. I'm reminded of the opening sentence of the Fourth Gospel, "In the beginning was the Word" — the Greek term for "Word" is Logos, which also signifies reason, idea, and rational or logical discourse.

What is an original creation of reason? To begin with, an original creation is the bringing into existence of something from nothing. To be sure, the elements of the created thing may have been there already; there was the land and the people, and their settlements and their several social organizations, as well as traditions of political thought and of government. But in none of these things by themselves or together was there power, let alone authority, to achieve it. What was needed was the endowment of an idea of reason with power and authority, transforming it into a powerful motive for political action. This idea is named in the very first sentence: "The laws of Nature and of Nature's God" which entitle every people to become a separate and equal state merely by declaring it. And by what means is this authority discovered? By reason only. It was not for nothing that the age in which this nation began has been called the Age of Reason. Universal Reason is the court that decides whether the act of independence of the 13 colonies was just. Nature's God does not preside in any Church or religious society, but in nature itself, and in the mind of every rational being, for all rational beings are creatures of nature. The court of reason is here and everywhere and beholden to no one.

There were, indeed, religious precedents to this idea. The very fact that the Congress met in Philadelphia, which was the preeminent city of Pennsylvania, founded by Quakers, who regarded truth as a common property, is indicative of the historical origins of the idea. But these precedents are not sufficient to explain it. What occurred in Philadelphia nearly two-and-one-half centuries ago was entirely new.

We must seek the originative power of the idea in the Age of Reason itself and in its central belief that the universe in which we exist is a moral universe, governed by laws. This central quality of the nature of things makes it possible to appeal to "The Law of Nature and Nature's God" as an authority above all other authorities. Reason is its active principle, and its self-revelation is like a light radiating from the universal intelligence, which is Nature itself, which shines into all natural things. Reason created the universe and established its laws. Hence, every rational being is able by itself to discover the origin and principle of nature and the nature of things, and in circumstances such as oppression by a tyrannous government, it becomes the ultimate court of appeal.

But what if the Age of Reason has passed, and with it the validity of the idea of a moral universe, what if rational beings can no longer appeal to the Laws of Nature and Nature's God? What if they are just another historical fashion? What if Nature is in fact no more than a random process, with neither beginning nor end nor purpose? Would this delegitimize the deed of the Continental Congress? Would it deprive the Declaration of Independence of any cogency or relevance?

I think not. For we remain a rational species, rational beings, who alone are responsible for our actions and alone capable of judging right from wrong, just from unjust, true from false. Appeals to reason become the ultimate means upon which those who are oppressed can rely when all other help fails. They are no less valid now than they were during the Enlightenment. Nature's God may have become silent, but reason continues and remains our only guide in life. The coming of age of each and every one of us is still to attain the age of reason, to become rational adults.

It has been claimed that one of the sources that the authors of the Declaration of Independence relied on was John Locke. In his "Second Treatise of Government," Locke introduces the notion of an appeal to heaven, and by it he imagined situations when oppressed citizens or groups of them have no recourse but to replace their government with another of their own making. Locke was imagining a situation of great risk where the die was cast, but the outcome uncertain. And there is no doubt that the members of the Continental Congress and their constituents faced such a situation in 1776. They were engaged in an undeclared war with Great Britain, which was a great empire with great power and immeasurable resources. There was no guarantee that they would succeed. In this circumstance, they had only the power of reason to guide them. That they succeeded must remain a cause of wonder.

All of this is sufficient reason to venerate the Declaration of Independence, along with its author or authors, and the Congress that enacted it. But in this case, the only right way to venerate them is to understand the document they bequeathed to us, to review its claims and its proof, and to do so rationally and critically and thereby to make it our act as well.

The Case for Independence

THE DECLARATION OF INDEPENDENCE as an act of Congress occurred on July 2, 1776, after being debated for more than a month. On July 3, 1776, John Adams reported this action to Abigail Adams, his wife.

"Yesterday the greatest Question was decided, which ever was debated in America, and a greater perhaps, never was or will be decided among Men. A Resolution was passed without one dissenting Colony "that these united Colonies, are, and of right ought to be free and independent States …"

A day later, Congress voted to adopt The Declaration of Independence. It had been drafted by a committee consisting of John Adams of Massachusetts, Benjamin Franklin of Pennsylvania, Thomas Jefferson of Virginia, Robert Livingston of New York, and Roger Sherman of Connecticut. Jefferson was the principal author of the draft. It was debated in Congress, revised, and adopted, and published as a formal announcement or proclamation. It presents the following argument justifying the action taken two days before.

First, it is noted that this action has historical precedent. There are occasions "in the course of human events," when a people find it necessary to "dissolve the political bands" that joined them to another people and assume "the separate and equal station to which the Laws of Nature and of Nature's God entitle them." Nevertheless, when such occasions occur, it is incumbent upon those who separate to state the reasons of their action. A "decent respect to the opinions of mankind" requires it. Without this rational ground of common understanding and agreement, the business of human society could not be conducted.

What follows is a theory of government in three clauses. The first asserts the self-evident truths of human equality and universal inalienable rights of life, liberty, and the pursuit of happiness. Next, Governments, which properly derive their powers from the consent of the governed, are obliged to secure these rights for all of them. Finally, when any government "becomes destructive of these ends" the people, whose consent established it in the first place, have the right "to alter or abolish it."

Next follows a word of caution. Prudence, a moral and political virtue, requires that "Governments long established should not be changed for light and transient causes." This is a counsel of caution or imperfection. It is often wiser to "bear the ills we gave than fly to others we know not of." Prudence advises "Be patient."

But patience has limits, and these limits have been transgressed by "a long train of abuses and usurpations" that are not random, but which reveal a common sinister purpose: namely, to establish an absolute despotism over the colonies. The evidence is conclusive.

Having stated in general the reasons for independence, the evidence is presented in detail. There follows a list of "injuries and usurpations" committed by the King and his ministers, "all having in direct object the establishment of an absolute Tyranny over these states." The list contains twenty-eight grievances that range over the following: interfering in the legislative processes of the states; ignoring their legislative actions; tampering with their elections, refusing to allow them, or not accepting their results; corrupting the administration of justice; pursuing a policy of militarization, and waging war against the people. The Congress has petitioned the King to end these oppressions "in the most humble terms," but to no avail. From all this it follows that "A Prince whose character is thus marked by every act which may define a Tyrant, is unfit to be the ruler of a free people."

It is stated also that the Congress has appealed to British people through their parliament, and to their "native Justice and Magnanimity" and kindred ties, all to no effect

The conclusion follows: "We, therefore, the Representatives of the United States of America, in General Congress, Assembled, appealing to the Supreme Judge of the world for the rectitude of our intentions, do, in the Name, and by the Authority of the good People of these Colonies, solemnly publish and declare, That these United Colonies are, and of Right ought to be Free and Independent States." The colonies no longer owe any allegiance to the British Crown, and all ties to the State of Great Britain and to its people are dissolved. They are now and hereafter free and independent states, free to wage war, to make peace, to enter into international treaties, and engage in commerce with other nations.

Note that by this unanimous declaration the thirteen states did not create one comprehensive state. Rather, by it, each state became sovereign and independent in its own right. Independence was their common endeavor and goal, and for this purpose they pledged to each other their lives, their fortunes, and their sacred honor. They were now engaged in a mutual endeavor.

The creation of a more perfect union between the states was still to come. Nevertheless, the act of independence was done, and it was irrevocable. And it brought into being a new political consciousness founded on irrefutable principles, among them, the principles of equality, and of the inalienable human rights of life, liberty, and the pursuit of happiness, and, finally, the principle that no government has legitimacy unless its only endeavor is to secure these rights for all of its people. To depart from this endeavor is to enter a path along that leads to tyranny.

Because the act of the Continental Congress declaring independence was an act of Reason it became a model all peoples could follow, and it established a right that all peoples could claim: the right of a people to political independence and by mutual consent to create their own government. It should be no surprise that this universal right of peoples could be the cause of chronic disorder in world history. For instance, it can lead to conflicts between peoples that claim the same land as their home, of which there are many current examples, and conflicts over what constitutes the identity of a people, and over what rights to accord those who do not meet the criteria of identity, and the problem of how to reconcile the right of peoples to be free and independent with the inalienable rights of individual persons to life, liberty, and the pursuit of happiness, which must be everywhere and always observed. Ever since the declaration, it has become the duty of our species to create and maintain a global society in which these irrevocable rights of peoples and of persons are faithfully maintained.

One could write a history of the world from July 4, 1776 to the present with these issues as its focus. But it would be without a conclusion, for that is more to come and we are not mere observers of the narrative but active participants in it, and our histories are only provisional, subject to revision.

More on Independence

I HAVE WRITTEN ABOUT the Declaration of Independence as though it were a perfect statement of principles. It was not.

Nor did it escape contemporary observers that the promoters of independence were shortsighted in the application of the principles of reason they espoused, and to that extent they were hypocrites. I will mention only one acute observer, Abigail Adams.

In a letter to John Adams, her husband and second U.S. president, written months before the Declaration was composed, she expressed doubts about their endeavor. She wondered how "the passion for Liberty" could really exist "in the Breasts of those who have been accustomed to deprive their fellow Creatures of theirs." She was referring to slavery.

And she had good reason for her doubt. In an early draft of the Declaration, Thomas Jefferson included a condemnation of King George III because he introduced slavery into the colonies, and he equates this with waging war against humanity itself: "He has waged cruel war against human nature itself," wrote Jefferson, "violating its most sacred rights of life & liberty in the persons of a distant people who never offended him, captivating & carrying them into slavery in another hemisphere, or to incur miserable death in their transportation thither."

This clause was deleted and replaced by another, which is arguably racist. It charges the King with exciting "domestic insurrections among us"; the immediate agents of these insurrections are not mentioned, but it is undoubtedly a reference to African slaves. In the same clause the King is blamed with causing "merciless Indian Savages to make war against the colonies," knowing that their method of waging war is indiscriminate killing "of all ages, sexes, and conditions."

Abigail Adams also counseled her husband that as he and his colleagues were at work fashioning a new code of laws for the colonies, "I desire you would Remember the Ladies," and she warned, "if particular care and attention is not paid to the Ladies, we are determined to foment a Rebellion, and will not hold ourselves bound by any laws in which we have no voice, or representation."

She rightly anticipated Elizabeth Cady Stanton and Susan B. Anthony and much more that has been done, and still needs to be done, to rectify the wrongs against women.

These things make clear that the people for whom the Declaration of Independence first spoke were, for the most part, white males who were by descent Englishmen, in short, "Wasps." We must be grateful that the idea of independence proved to be more powerful than the prejudices of many of its original proponents, and along with it the rights of all sorts and conditions of human beings.

And it hardly needs be said that the struggle to realize these ideas in all their purity is not ended, nor is its outcome certain, which is all the more reason why we must constantly renew them in our minds and hold them sacred.

Before ending this discussion of independence, there remains this question: What sort of form of government did the proponents of "independence" want to create? A Democracy or a Republic are the usual answers. But they are not the same form, so which is it? Historically, democracy originated in ancient Athens; republic signified the polity of ancient Rome, before Caesar's coup.

The simplest, indeed literal, definition of "Democracy" is the rule of the people. Greek political theory distinguished between three kinds of government in terms of the number of those who rule: one, few, or many — or monarchy, aristocracy or democracy.

Plato, who witnessed the downfall of democracy in Greece, took a dim view of it. His fear, which was confirmed by events, was that democracy was unstable, and that it led inevitably to tyranny, which he considered the greatest political evil of all. A classical democracy consisted of one ruling body: the assembly of the people, who made laws and administered justice, and decided on all public affairs, domestic and foreign, including declaring war.

In a direct democracy, all decisions are made by vote of the people. But Plato saw that the people at large were often not motivated to act by reason, but by their passions, which were aroused by political orators, who appealed to their prejudices rather than to their rational good sense. Moreover, since there was no higher rule than the assembly of the people, there was no rule of fundamental law, nor basic principles of right that might act as a safeguard against mass feeling, which fed upon resentments and prejudices.

The people's assembly seemed to Plato the perfect seedbed for clever demagogues to plant their self-serving ideas and thereby gain power. They were mere flatterers of the people and patrons of their own egos.

This was not the sort of democracy that Pericles practiced, but it remained a constant threat even during that golden age of ancient Greece. There is no doubt a dark aspect of democracy, which we are witnessing today. It is fed by populist prejudices and crude demagoguery, and it is not being effectively resisted.

In any case, to conclude, a form of government may be described as democratic if it maintains the principle of universal suffrage.

A republic is also a government of the people inasmuch as it rejects the heredity rights of a ruling family or of nobility in general. But it otherwise tends toward elitism.

It founds government on a fundamental law that cannot or must not be transgressed either by any individual or by the unanimous voice of the people. This law may be inherent in the nature of things or it may be established by the people through their elected representatives, as was the case with the American Constitution.

Which introduces another feature of republican government: It is government by representatives, who although elected by the people, they are also bound by the rule of law even when that law requires that they act contrary to public sentiment. In addition, public officials are expected to exhibit all the qualities of civic virtue in their actions: prudence, temperance, courage and justice. It promotes government by a moral elite.

To conclude, the United States of American is not a pure democracy; rather it is a democratic republic. Hence Jefferson, who was well read in the history of politics, named his political party The Democratic Republican Party, which stood against the Federalists.

Postscript: As the historian Pauline Maier has observed, the Declaration of Independence has become a sacred text, which is all the more reason that it be read carefully and critically. Her book, *American Scripture* (New York: Vintage Press, 1998) is a readable and reliable guide.

Questioning Common Sense

Thomas Paine (1737-1809) was a political activist, revolutionary, and pamphleteer. English by birth, he became an American citizen and a citizen of the French Republic by choice and played a key role in their respective revolutions. He is best remembered for his revolutionary writings, *Common Sense, The Rights of Man,* and *The Age of Reason.*

Common Sense was published in February 1776 and was an immediate best seller. It is credited with having provided direction and purpose to members of the Continental Congress as they deliberated their way towards independence. It did this by identifying the available options, namely, independence or reconciliation, and by giving cogent reasons for choosing the former instead of the latter. But Common Sense is above all a call to action, and after almost two-and-one half centuries its passion is undiminished and its message timely.

> "O ye that love mankind! Ye that dare
> oppose, not only the tyranny, but the
> tyrant, stand forth! Every spot of the old
> world is overrun with oppression. Freedom
> hath been hunted round the globe. Asia,
> and Africa, have long expelled her. Europe
> regards her like a stranger, and England

hath given her warning to depart. *O! receive the fugitive, and prepare in time an asylum for mankind.*"

His vision of America as "an asylum for mankind" is noble, worthy of honor, but, even more, a never-ending imperative for all Americans, nor more so than today, when it is being cruelly ignored.

Scattered occurrences of armed conflict between the American Colonies and Great Britain began in 1770 most notably with the Boston Massacre and continued intermittently culminating in general war. On July 3, 1775, following the Battles of Lexington and Bunker Hill, the Continental Congress appointed George Washington commander-in-chief of the Colonial armies, and two days later declared that a state of war existed between the Colonies and the British government. Congress described it as a civil war not a revolution, thus acknowledging the continuing bond of the colonies with Great Britain and the British people.

When the Congress met in 1776 it considered only two options: reconciliation with Great Britain or independence. Looking back, it may seem that the choice was obvious, but it did not seem so then. One of the so-called "founding fathers," John Dickinson of Delaware, a highly respected member of Congress, did not believe that the colonies were ready for independence. He worried that the differences between them, chief among them slavery, would continue to divide them and eventually lead to conflict and civil war between the states. He counseled negotiations leading towards greater autonomy. He absented himself from Congress rather than vote on the question of independence and, when the Declaration was adopted, he refused to sign it. He resigned his seat in Congress and enlisted in the militia as a private. One year later, in recognition of independence, he freed his slaves. Later, he played a major role in drafting the Articles of Confederation.

Paine begins *Common Sense* by distinguishing between human society and government. Society is spontaneous and natural, but fragile, unable to sustain itself, which necessitates the creation of government. Government, then, is a "necessary evil"; what makes society fragile and unenduring is the incapacity of individuals to maintain the purity of motives and the friendliness that originally brought them together. Paine appears to follow Rousseau who believed that all men are born innocent and become corrupt when they enter into civil society. Thus, he compares a person's entry into society to the biblical Fall: corruption follows, and with it the necessity of mutual restraints, of laws and governments to enforce them. "Government, like dress, is the badge of lost innocence." But the process of corruption is incremental; it accelerates and increases as states increase their domains and enlarge their governments, which stand apart from and above those they rule, so that it becomes arbitrary and harsh.

Yet the only legitimate purpose of government, large or small, is to preserve the liberty and security of its citizens, to which they have a natural right. Governments that ignore this fundamental purpose and seek some other goal, for example, glory or empire, become tyrannical; they must be resisted.

Paine acknowledges that efforts have been made to reform civil government, with modest success. He admits that the British have done more than other peoples to reform government. He offers faint praise for the English constitution, which served in its time as a successful antidote to absolutism and the tyranny of monarchs by creating a mixed government that combined the powers of king, nobles, and the people into a single system of countervailing forces. But all this soon degenerated into a medley of tyrannies, "a house divided."

This is his argument against the English constitution: power corrupts, and even if the mixed English constitution divides the power of government into three parts, each with its constitutional right, each will endeavor to maintain its power to a certain degree unchecked, yet if neither is able to subdue the others, then the establishment of three opposing tyrannies is the inevitable outcome; any hope that government will work for the welfare of the people diminishes. Stalemate follows and chronic injustice.

When government becomes corrupt, the best option is to separate oneself from it. Independence is the only rational option; the hope for reconciliation is an illusion.

The question remains whether we should expect anything better from the present American government. To be sure, the hereditary rights of the monarch and the noble aristocracy have been abolished here. The offices of government are open to all and are filled by popular elections. But the power of government is the same, whether British or American, whether in a president or a king, and power, now as then, corrupts. We have all become daily observers of how this happens.

We assure ourselves that the separation of powers prescribed by our constitution is a reliable system of checks and balances and this assurance persuades us that the common good will be served, as though our government were a "machine that runs by itself." Is this assurance justified? What if, instead of checks and balances, the different branches stand incorrigibly opposed, and instead of a well-functioning machine, there is gridlock caused by the attempted tyranny of one part of government over the others? What if the separation of powers has brought us only an unending cycle of action and reaction? And if this should happen, what remedy is available to us, the people?

But I have strayed from my purpose, which is historical not homiletical. The founders were not unaware of the difficult tasks facing them, chief among them, how to design a system of government that was self-regulating and immune from corruption. John Adams was well aware of this and he proposed a remedy.

John Adams on Government

THOMAS PAINE AND JOHN ADAMS REPRESENT opposite types in manners, motives and ideas. But they were united in a common cause, brought together by the force of circumstance, which they seized as a political opportunity of great historical moment. Through many trials and not without error, and despite their opposite tendencies, these two complemented each other and comprised the complex and often bewildering American political genius.

Paine was a populist and a skeptic. His populism is evident in his vision of America as a refuge and asylum for all people in search of a better life. Yet he also harbored doubts that any society could rise to this high calling, for he believed that society corrupts.

Adams was no less skeptical than Paine, and he was a more consistent moral skeptic. He doubted that a mere assembly of people, guided only by a common sentiment, could establish justice—which is a Populist ideal. Therefore, the very framework of government, Adams believed, must be designed so that it counteracts mere sentiment by channeling human energy and ambition into rational institutional pathways that are determined to be reliable and just. He called this form of government, Republicanism.

Populism and Republicanism are the two poles of the American political system.

The central idea of Adams' republican theory is "the rule of law." In *Thoughts on Government*, published in May 1776, he swept aside the long tradition of political thought of laying out the merits and demerits of the various types of governments: monarchy, aristocracy or democracy, and called immediately for the creation of a republic, which was to be "an empire of laws, not of men."

By "laws," he meant not only the fundamental laws that establish a civil government and prescribe its organization (the law of constitutions), but also laws enacted by legitimate legislative bodies—in sum, the whole body of law.

To bring all this about, he proposed the acceptance of three principles.

First, the principle of representation prescribes that the legislative body of government be made up of persons chosen for their moral fitness, rather than their popular appeal. Hence, legislative power must be deputed "from the many to a few of the most wise and good." This may be described as Adams' anti-populist or elitist principle.

However, he required that the legislative body be proportional to population, that legislators be elected annually by the people, and that a legislature "be in miniature an exact portrait of the people at large."

"It should think, feel, reason and act like them," and, overall, "serve the common interest." Even here, however, he moralizes. The "common interest" is not a collection of everyday wishes and desires shared among a majority of the people, he wrote, but a deep passion for "the noblest principles and generous affections of our nature."

Second, there must be a complete separation of the three powers of government: legislative, executive and judicial. The reasons he gives have to do with function. The legislative process must be open to view to any who care to observe it; laws must not be made in secret. On the other hand, the executive must be able to act in secret, even though all its actions must be recorded, and officials held accountable for their decisions and actions. Membership of the judiciary requires a special competence that goes far beyond any legal competence required of those in the other branches of government.

Third, the legislature must consist of more than one body, so that there is a system of checks and balances within the legislative process itself; this policy is reinforced by the right of review by an independent judiciary.

****

Adams' republican idea appears to give priority to the legislative branch of government, for it has the power to make law, which is the primary expression of the sovereignty of a nation. Yet he also favored a strong executive possessing a right of legislative veto to counterbalance it.

Adams expressed the hope that government would be able to cause "the happiness of society," of happiness infused with virtue. This is not a novel thought. What does he mean by it? Happiness is a feeling, and as far as I know, only individuals have feelings. Yet, individuals in society have feelings, and they are infectious, and this applies especially to feelings of content or discontent with respect to government. If an overwhelming majority of citizens believe that the laws are just and that public officials justly apply them, then that civil society may be described as happy or content.

But Adams conveys a more vibrant feeling than contentment. He was by all accounts a sober and often somber man, and very straight-laced, yet in spite of all of this, his revolutionary writings convey a near utopian excitement. Although his prescription that a government achieves happiness through an impartial administration of laws is not new, he thought that the real possibility of achieving it had been reached in America, something never achieved anywhere before. And he celebrated that moment.

He also believed that the empire of laws about to be established would be an empire of liberty: a society voluntarily shaped and constituted by the free choice of the people, who agree to submit to the rule of laws, enacted and executed by its constitutionally chosen representatives.

Furthermore, the laws, and the representatives who make and execute them, must serve the public interest or public good. And what is that? They must be laws that "suit the nature of justice," which requires serving the public interest and not the private interests of a privileged few. Laws must be proper expressions of the will of the whole people, of their common right. They must be enacted in public, and the proponents and opponents of proposed laws must debate them using rational discourse.

In short, reason and virtue must prevail over passion, greed and resentment.

Such was the system of government that Adams hoped would be established in America. It would be a union of independent states, each with its own republican constitution. And in a quiet and modest way Adams imagined that in time the center of the world empire would migrate from Europe to America, although only for a time, not forever.

The First American Confederacy

Before the United States of America achieved "a more perfect union" through the ratification of the Constitution of 1787, it was a Confederacy. This word itself, which became notorious because of the secession by seven southern states in 1860 and the horrendous war that followed between north and south, has an uncontroversial meaning.

The Oxford English Dictionary defines a confederacy as "a union by league or contract between persons, bodies of men, or states, for mutual support or joint action; a league, alliance, compact." The word is a compound consisting of a prefix (con, from the Latin word, *cum*, i.e., with) and a stem (federate, whose Latin root is *foedus*, that is, covenant, contract, or agreement; federate means to join by agreement, contract, or covenant; uniting in a common purpose). Politically, a Confederacy is a union of autonomous societies or states; the purpose of confederation is public welfare.

The Articles of Confederation were adopted in 1781 by representatives of the 13 American states, formerly colonies of Great Britain. They had declared their independence from Great Britain five years before, and following a long war in defense of it, had achieved victory over British forces at Yorktown. The Articles were supposed to achieve a "perpetual union" of all the states: New Hampshire, Massachusetts, Rhode Island, Connecticut, New York, New Jersey, Pennsylvania, Delaware, Maryland, Virginia, North Carolina, South Carolina and Georgia.

It should be recalled that the Declaration of Independence declared that the 13 colonies were thereafter 13 free and independent states. Sovereignty resided in each state and not in the Continental Congress, nor did it reside in a new nation, the United States of America. The Articles of Confederation did not propose to change this, but only to establish a union between the states; to be sure, a perpetual one.

But, as the historian Gordon Wood has observed, in 1776, there was little if any thought of this union becoming "a single republic, one community with one pervasive public interest" (Wood, The Creation of the American Republic, p. 356).

The independence of the colonies was decided by war, and The Treaty of Paris, which formally ended hostilities between Great Britain and the United States, also acknowledged the sometime colonies to be, individually, free, independent, sovereign states.

Yet the founders fervently believed that something new, and monumentally historic was being brought into the world: a permanent union of states dedicated to the principles of liberty and equality.

The Articles of Confederation and, later, The Constitution of the United States adopted in 1787, and the Civil War, which happened almost a century later, were decisive moments in the long achievement of this goal. The goal still beckons; it is an almost mystical goal. The Union forever! Which is why the Articles and Constitution must still be read, and their histories recalled, for they are records in the making and remaking of the United States, which remains a task for us, today and hereafter.

****

The Articles of Confederation aimed at a compromise between independence and union. The first article establishes that henceforth the states comprise a Confederacy called

The United States of America. The second article asserts that, nevertheless, "each state retains its sovereignty, freedom and independence." Yet their sovereignty is limited by the agreements spelled out in the articles that follow.

In the third article, the states agree to join together in a common and mutual defense. Any threat to the liberty or welfare of one will be regarded as a threat to all and will be met with a united response.

The fourth article declares that the right of citizenship in one state entails the same right in them all. This right applies, however, only to the free inhabitants of a state, not to "paupers, vagabonds, and fugitives from justice," and, although not named, it does not apply to slaves. The self-evident truth of equality asserted in the Declaration was ignored.

The principle of "full faith and credit" also applied between the states. According to this principle, each state must recognize all "records, acts, and judicial procedures" of every other state. This applies to all public documents, statutes, and judicial actions in each state. This provision was retained in the Constitution, and it was applied to slave laws (see Article II, section 2, paragraph 3), which became the cause of ongoing controversy that was finally decided by civil war and by the adoption of the 13th Amendment, which abolished slavery.

Article five of the Articles created the Congress of the United States. It was to be a unicameral assembly of delegates, each state represented by at least two and by no more than seven delegates, the number and manner of their selection to be determined by each state legislature. Whatever the size of its delegation, each state would have only one vote. The right of free speech was to be observed in all congressional debates.

Articles six through nine gave Congress the sole authority to engage in diplomacy, to enact international treaties, to wage war, and to make peace. No state or group of them had the right to enter into a treaty with other states or a foreign government, or to restrict trade, or establish tariffs. Every state had the responsibility to maintain an armed militia and, in some instances, naval forces, but without the authority to declare or wage war, which belonged only to Congress. The states were to maintain armed forces only for the common defense. Officers of Colonel and above were appointed by Congress; lower ranks by state legislatures. The Congress only had power to regulate money. It also served as the ultimate court of appeals in disputes between the states.

Article nine also established "A Committee of the States," made up of one delegate from each state with the authority to acquire a managerial staff, subject to congressional approval. This committee and its staff became the executive department of government. It was to be headed up by a president appointed annually by the committee. The president was not a chief executive, but rather a chair of the board, and was permitted to serve in that office for only one in three successive years.

Succeeding articles dealt with the appropriation of funds to the states ("in proportion to the number of white inhabitants"), the congressional calendar, the duration of its recesses (no more than six months), and the conduct of business when Congress is not in session, and the recourse to secrecy in matters concerning treaties, foreign alliances, and military operations. The Articles extend an open invitation to Canada to joint the confederation of states. The final article, number 13, required that every state observe the articles of confederation, unless exempted by congress and the unanimous agreement of all of the state legislatures.

The Articles were not long adopted when they were judged to be inadequate. They left too much sovereignty in the states, and failed to provide enough union. This led to the desire to create "a more perfect union," which will be discussed in the next essay.

VICTOR NUOVO

Constitutionalism

CONSTITUTIONALISM IS A THEORY of government by the rule of law. It is not a mere expression of the wishes and desires of a monarch, or the whims and fancies of a demagogue, or a legal device fashioned to serve the special interests of the rich, but a fundamental law or constitution pertaining to the whole nation, individually and collectively.

A constitution is a set of basic rules by which a nation is organized and governed. It may be written or unwritten. The British Constitution, if it may be called such, is largely unwritten, and, in any case, is rooted in dubious traditions vaguely defined, and is mired in privilege.

In contrast, the Constitution of the United States of America consists of a single, relatively short document that prescribes an entire system of government and its practices as well as the rights and duties of its officials and its people together with the means of amending it. It is the first of its kind in recorded history and also the longest lasting, and, since its ratification in 1787, it has become a model and precedent for new nations and for old nations seeking renewal. It is something in which we can all take pride, but proper pride must be rooted in knowledge and critical understanding.

The terms "constitution" and "fundamental law" convey this meaning. To found or constitute a thing is to give it form and existence; it is an act of original creation. The process of framing and adopting the constitution by a convention of representatives selected by the people of each state, and its subsequent ratification by the states in the same way concluded with the coming into existence of a new entity, a nation such as The United States of America.

Once ratified, the Constitution became the "the supreme law of the land." This process is not hidden in mystery; although the sessions of the Constitutional Convention were closed, the issues considered and the arguments made for and against are known, and were recorded in the notes and diaries of the delegates. Ratification by the states was an open process. Overall, the process was one of rational argument and compromise, which is as good as it gets in politics.

Article VI of the Constitution declares that all laws enacted in accordance with its articles and all treaties entered into under its authority thereby also become law, so that this nation remains in perpetuity a nation under law.

By what authority did this happen? One need only read the Preamble for an answer:

"We the people of the United States, in Order to form a more perfect Union, establish Justice, insure domestic Tranquility, provide for the common Defense, promote the general Welfare, and secure the Blessings of Liberty to ourselves and our Posterity,

so ordain and establish this Constitution for the United Stated of America."

****

This Constitution was enacted and it purposes prescribed by the authority of the "People of the United States,' not by the states, acting through their respective legislatures, but by the People at large. The People are its authors and enactors. They claim for themselves this sovereign right, and they recognize no other authority in heaven or on earth that might challenge it, and indeed there is none. By the People's act of ordaining and establishing the Constitution, The United States of America became a nation, and the People, its sovereign. It was a magnificent act of self-creation, and it forever negated the once prevailing prejudice that government required a monarch or a privileged few or a god to establish and reign over it.

But there is more. By the very act through which the People declared themselves sovereign they also subjected themselves to this supreme law. They became subjects of their own self-prescribed law, whose rule is stated in the Constitution.

Thus, "The People of the United States" is not an anarchic aggregation of individuals, nor a populist crowd, nor an unruly mob. It is a sovereign person, eminently rational, a self-regulating body that exists over time under a fundamental law instituted by itself, which all of the people are duty bound "to preserve, protect, and defend."

Finally, the goals and purposes of the Constitution are clearly stated: Justice, Domestic Tranquility, the Common Defense, the General Welfare, and the guarantee of the Blessings of Liberty to this and all succeeding generations. The list covers everything of political and moral value.

****

The United States of America is a four-dimensional entity. It has a place—this broad land and the sky above it—and it has a history that extends through time. And we, the people of the United States, are its citizens. In this era of identity politics, this should be our primary identity as individuals and communities, so that we can unite as free and equal persons under one law as one nation.

This is not to say that we should regale ourselves in chauvinist bigotry, but live together as citizens bound by the same law, impartial in its application, always welcoming to immigrants and dedicated to equality, justice, liberty, public safety, and to the welfare for all.

When I had come this far in writing this essay, I paused to reflect on what it all meant, and it dawned upon me that I had discovered the "very idea of the United States of America." I am surely not the first person to have made this discovery, a vast multitude have already done so, many much earlier in life. But the idea is the same and valid nevertheless—better late than never.

I recalled that this law and its first enactment, its ratification and successive amendments, is the product not of some founding genius but of ordinary fallible human beings. It is the product of the deliberations of committees of persons like you and me, each with private interests, vain, selfish, beset by prejudices and resentments, yet capable or rational deliberation which produced a law that has slowly and at times painfully been revised and enlarged. In that process it has become more inclusive so that that the People of the United States now includes not just individuals of one gender or race or ethnicity or culture or sexual preference or religion, but a mixture of all, native born and immigrant, a People ever growing more inclusive and more equal who together are, by their acceptance of this law, irrevocably dedicated to establishing justice, insuring domestic peace, uniting in a common defense, promoting the general welfare, and securing the blessings of liberty for all generations now and to come.

This Constitution is our common heritage. It is ours by right. And we are all duty bound to keep it. Or we may ignore it and perish.

Federalism

RICHARD HOFSTADTER, FROM WHOSE BOOK *The American Political Tradition* I have taken the theme of this series has observed that the framers of the Constitution were by and large moral pessimists and that their pessimism led to the outcome of their labors. They believed that most if not all men were selfish, resentful, more often driven by passion rather than by cool impartial rational judgment—I use the term "men" here, because the framers were under the misapprehension that the business of government was solely men's business.

In any case, they believed that men were not disposed by nature to respect the rights of others or to put the common good above their own private interests, and that even the best of men, individuals who were regarded as morally upright in their day-to-day behavior, seemed to lose all moral constraint when part of a crowd.

James Madison summed it up in his comment that "had every Athenian citizen been a Socrates, every Athenian assembly would still have been a mob."

Madison's remark was profoundly ironic for he was well aware that it was an Athenian popular assembly that had condemned Socrates to death for questioning popular wisdom. He believed that all popular assemblies were by nature "intemperate," prone to vindictive madness, which in the end is self-destructive. According to this point of view, men are not by nature political animals, as Aristotle supposed, rather, as Hobbes believed, they become such by necessity.

The Framers of the Constitution embraced this opinion. They desired a strong central government that would be immune to human selfishness, populist enthusiasm, and the pride of the individual states, one founded on "republican principles." They hoped, perhaps believed, that high office would ennoble the individuals who occupy them. It was a vain hope, but essential if government is to work at all.

****

The Constitution was drafted and approved by an assembly of delegates that met in Philadelphia from May 25 until September 17, 1787. It was then transmitted to the states for ratification. Article VII of the Constitution stipulated that at least nine of the thirteen states must ratify it before it could become law.

Almost two years would pass before this was achieved. During this period, three of the framers, Alexander Hamilton, John Jay and James Madison published newspaper articles promoting the Constitution and explaining its principles. These articles since gathered together are known to us as The Federalist Papers, which has become a world classic. Thomas Jefferson gave it high praise calling it "the best commentary on the principles of government, which was ever written." This is especially noteworthy because Jefferson was not a Federalist.

Of the three authors, the papers written by Madison are most relevant to our theme. In Federalist Papers no. 39, he summarized the "republican principles" that he desired to become the foundation of the American constitutional system. There are three principles: first, all government officials, executive and legislative, must be selected directly or indirectly by the people; second, their offices are for a limited duration; third, members of the judicial branch shall hold office without limit, although on good behavior, which gives the judiciary an advantage over the legislative and executive branches of government and an immunity from popular sentiment. They are supposed to be foremost guardians of the Constitution. A fourth may be added to these, the principle of representation, which prescribes that the business of government be conducted not by committees of the whole but by representatives of the people.

The underlying principle of these four is the separation of powers. The founder who championed this principle was John Adams. It was his opinion that separation of powers was necessary to avoid the abuse of power in any one office, but also to avoid the pressure of mass assemblies. Adams stated and defended his theory of government in a long scholarly work, "A Defence of the Constitutions," first published in January 1787. It served as a guidebook to delegates to the Constitutional Convention. It was Adams's genius and moral outlook, not Jefferson's, that presided over the framers of the Constitution.

In this respect, the Constitution differs from the Declaration of Independence, which Jefferson authored. The Declaration is founded on the premise of the rights of the people. The Constitution is founded on the principle of the rule of law; it makes no mention of rights, an omission that would be rectified by the first ten amendments, the Bill of Rights.

Together these two documents represent the two poles of our system of government. Each is necessary. Without rights, the rule of law becomes oppressive; without law, a system of rights devolves into anarchy. Tyranny and anarchy are the two extremes of our political existence; they are ever-present tendencies, in constant tension. The aim of republicanism is to negotiate a safe path between them, using a system of checks and balances as its navigational guide.

The American Republic, then, is a complex affair of opposing systems, expressed in our two founding documents. Madison explains this also in Federalist Papers, no. 39. At first glance, this complexity is confusing, but as one reflects upon it, it seems a work of genius.

Madison observes that our system is based on two political entities: a nation and a collection of independent states. This diversity is also expressed in our two legislative bodies, the House of Representatives and the Senate. Members of the House are chosen by the direct popular vote, apportioned according to districts whose boundaries are determined by population. The Senate assigns two seats to each state, regardless of their population; it is based on the principle of the equality of the states, regardless of their size and wealth.

The election of the president is by popular vote of the nation, but filtered through the Electoral College. Here too there is a playing off, as it were, of the nation and the states. The Electoral College, proportioned to each state, chooses the President, and it is not bound by the rule of majority so that it is possible that the candidate who received the smaller popular vote might become president.

Whether this system is just, is a moot question, which I am not qualified to answer. The Electoral College was supposed to base its decision on the moral qualities of the candidates. This may have been the hope of the framers of the Constitution, but if so, it was a false hope.

The Federalist Papers, consisting of 85 newspaper articles, were published under the name of a fictitious author: Publius, a Latin word, signifying a representative of the People. Alexander Hamilton wrote most of them (51), followed by James Madison (29), and John Jay (5). A convenient edition is published in paperback by Oxford World Classics. Every household should have a copy.

Anti-Federalism

IN THE POLITICAL DEBATE about the Constitution, its supporters labeled themselves "Federalists," although they might better have called themselves "nationalists," for they favored a strong national government rather than a loose federation of states. Among the founders, Washington, Adams, Hamilton, and Madison were Federalists, and a strong central government was their goal. On the other side of this debate stood Anti-Federalists. The term was coined in 1787 as an odious label, applied to any and all who opposed adoption of the Constitution.

The debate over the Constitution lasted three years, from the time that the Constitutional Convention was first convened until its ratification by all 13 states — from May 1787 until May 1790. There is an abundant record of it in notebooks and diaries of participants, newspaper articles, and speeches in public assemblies, and these have been preserved and reprinted in scholarly and popular editions. The opinions of the Anti-Federalists are therefore as accessible to us as those of the Federalists. They are worth attending to, for issues they raised are still current, and in some respects unsettled.

One of them concerned the legality of the Constitution. Anti-Federalists noted that the Constitutional

Convention was originally convened by Congress to consider revising the *Articles of Confederation*, which was then the official constitution of the United States. It was charged that the delegates ignored this directive and chose to make a new beginning exceeding the authority of Congress. The Constitution they produced acknowledged "The People of the United States" as the sole authority to establish it as law. As I noted in a previous essay, the Preamble of the constitution performs an act of self-creation, "The People of the United States of America" declare themselves sovereign, and their union a sovereign nation.

But one may ask, by what authority did they do this? If I may take the liberty of responding for the Federalists, I can imagine them dismissing the question as impertinent, "One might as well ask by what authority God created the world." It is enough that God has this originative power. The people of the United States had a similar authority and right, not to create worlds, but to form themselves into a nation, their nation, and to give it a fundamental law. This is the power of covenant, a principle of natural right.

The Anti-Federalists did not deny this sort of power, and this natural right. The problem for them is that that act of self-creation had already been done, 13 times. The states already had their own constitutions, and by their own declaration were free and sovereign entities, self-founded and independent. The Constitution negated these actions. To be sure, their declaration of independence was jointly made, but it did not create a new sovereign nation, rather 13 sovereign states united in a common cause. The Anti-Federalists worried that the Constitution would negate the sovereignty of the states, violating their independence and their liberty.

Moreover, they suspected that "The People of the United States" was a mere fiction, invented to subvert the authority of the states. This was not an idle suspicion, and I suspect that many of us, would be hard pressed to relieve it by giving a full and cogent explanation of the origin and meaning of the term, and even more important, the right and power of the entity that it connotes.

Furthermore, it was argued that the proposed Constitution made no provision for individual rights. This was a criticism raised by those of a Jeffersonian persuasion. In this respect, the Constitution appeared to ignore the self-evident truth appealed to in the Declaration of Independence, the right of every individual to life, liberty and the pursuit of happiness. This deficiency was quickly acknowledged and rectified. The Bill of Rights, consisting of the first ten amendments to the Constitution, was adopted by Congress on September 25, 1789, and sent to the States. It was ratified on December 15, 1791. Madison drafted the Bill, incorporating into it rights proposed by Anti-Federalists.

Anti-Federalists also raised questions concerning representation. The Constitution established two legislative bodies, The House of Representatives and the Senate. The House was to consist of delegations from each state proportional to their population. The size of the population of each state was to be equal to the number of free persons dwelling in each state, including indentured servants, plus 3/5 of all others not free — that is slaves. For purposes of representation, Slaves counted as 3/5 of a person, but not as citizens, for they had been denied the right to vote, were not free persons. They were regarded as property. The effect of this rule was to give slave states an advantage in congressional representation over those that were not. For example, according to the census of 1790, Virginia had a population of 747,000 of which 292,000 were slaves, contrasted to Pennsylvania with a population of 443,000 including only 3,707 slaves.

    The Senate posed other problems of representation. It was a select body, consisting of two senators from each state originally chosen by their respective state legislators — the 17th Amendment, adopted in 1912, required the election of senators by popular vote. This gave a disproportional representation to states with small populations. Some Anti-Federalists feared that the Senate would become an elitist body, that it would lead to the establishment of a noble class, a clear violation of the principle of equality. Their fear was enlarged by the fact that the terms of Senators were six years. As a general rule, Anti-Federalists preferred that the offices of government be renewed every year.

    Anti-Federalists worried about the office of the President and its executive powers.

They expressed the fear that the office was "a monarchy in the making." All that was lacking was succession by heredity. The current quarrel over the President's power to declare a national emergency and appropriate funds disregarding Congress suggests that the fear was not unadvised. The current fear of autocracy is not ill-advised.

Finally, Anti-Federalists opposed the appointment of Justices of the Supreme Court to life terms. And because justices were nominated by the President, they feared that their power could become an extension of the executive power of the President.

Postscript: A comprehensive body of Anti-Federalist documents has been collected and critically edited by the late Herbert Storing and published in seven volumes by the University of Chicago Press in 1981. Volume 1 contains an excellent introduction by Professor Storing. A selection of papers gathered from Storing's collection was published in 1985, edited by Murray Dry of Middlebury College and is available in paperback. Another handy collection of Anti-Federalist discourses also based on Storing's collection but with additional material is *The Anti-Federalism Papers* and *The Constitutional Convention Debates*, edited by Ralph Ketcham, Signet Classics.

Founding Brothers

IT IS NOW NO LONGER APPROPRIATE to use the expression "Founding Fathers" when referring to the founders of this nation. Its use was once meant to put them in a class above the people, to present them as venerable, whereas, we have come to realize that they, like us, were "human, all too human", flawed, and full of foibles. Besides, the expression smacks of patriarchalism, which is vile. "Founding Brothers", the title of a noted historical study of them by Joseph Ellis, has become the accepted expression. It has a better pedigree, for the founders used the expression "band of brothers" to refer to themselves. Of course, they were all male, a significant deficiency.

Among its younger members, notably Hamilton, Jefferson, Madison, and Burr, this band was beset by rivalry, jealousy, envy, and even fratricide. It is now well known that on July 11, 1804, Aaron Burr inflicted a mortal wound on Alexander Hamilton in a duel on the Heights of Weehawken, New Jersey. One is reminded of another tale of two brothers that led to fratricide, of Cain and Abel, but, although Burr came to bear the mark of Cain, he was no villain, nor was Hamilton a saint. They were ordinary men, gifted, but also driven by vain passions and ambition and uncontrolled rivalry. The event might be described as an American tragedy. I'm not sure that Lin-Manuel Miranda has portrayed it so in his play, *Hamilton,* in any case, while his play is justly praised for its drama and music, it is not reliable history, and should be considered for what it is, a work of the imagination, entertaining and edifying, but nonetheless a fiction.

Of the four just named, Aaron Burr, Jr. had the most distinguished ancestry. His maternal grandfather was Jonathan Edwards, who is most remembered as a religious revivalist, a leader of the Great Awakening, author of the famous or infamous sermon "Sinners in the Hand of an Angry God", but who was also, like his predecessor Cotton Mather, a philosopher of no mean ability, and an empirical naturalist. He died from complications resulting from a smallpox vaccination, to which he voluntarily submitted to encourage others to do the same. This occurred shortly after he assumed the presidency of The College of New Jersey (since renamed, Princeton University). He opposed slavery and had earlier served as a missionary to Mohawk Indians residing in Western Massachusetts, desiring not merely to convert them to Christianity, but thereby to include them in American society. Aaron Burr, Sr., Burr's father, was also a President of The College of New Jersey, which he attended, graduating at the early age of 17. Aaron Burr, Jr. opposed slavery. He was also an early advocate of the education of women. He read and admired the works of Mary Wollstonecraft, the author of *A Vindications of the Rights of Women*, and with that as a guide he oversaw the education of his daughter Theodosia, about whom I will have more to say in my next essay. He had abandoned the religion of his fathers.

Hamilton had a humbler heritage. Born out of wedlock in the Caribbean island of Nevis, and orphaned while still a child, he was a precocious youth, whose intelligence and brilliance attracted a circle of benefactors and sponsors. They arranged for him to attend King's College in New York (now Columbia University).

Hamilton and Jefferson were political opponents belonging to opposing parties. Jefferson preferred a decentralized system based on an agrarian economy. Hamilton favored a strong central government. He was also the founder of American capitalism and he promoted industrial growth and commerce. All three opposed slavery, although in this instance, Jefferson's hypocrisy becomes most evident. The historian Joseph Ellis cites Jefferson's own census of his household, or as Jefferson termed it, "my family". It consisted of eleven "free whites" and ninety-three slaves, "two of whom were his own children".

The cause of the animosity between Hamilton and Burr is uncertain. Hamilton had the unfortunate habit of being a loudmouth, especially when speaking of people he didn't like, or who were in his way. He accused Burr of certain "despicable acts". Just what he was referring to is a matter of speculation. Gore Vidal wrote a novel about Burr, entitled Burr; he conjectured that Hamilton was alluding to an unsubstantiated rumor that he had committed incest. But it is a mere conjecture, that has dramatic value. Yet, unlike Miranda, who produced Hamilton after reading only one recent biography, Vidal read widely in the sources, and his vast learning informs his art. The novel is worth reading, yet no one should forget that it also is fiction.

Politically, Burr and Jefferson, were political allies and ran on the same ticket, but they were also rivals. In the presidential election of 1800, they tied for the most votes in the electoral college for the presidency. The practice then was that the top vote getter would be President, and the next, Vice-President. But there was no top vote getter; although there was a prior understanding that the Presidency should go to Jefferson. It was up to Congress to decide; they chose Jefferson, with Hamilton's encouragement.

Hamilton let it be known that he considered Burr dangerous. But he might have said the same about Jefferson. For Jefferson's party favored a less centralized association of states, and Jefferson was less worried about the possibility of armed conflict between the states. Jefferson was no admirer of Hamilton; but he had a greater animosity towards Burr. Unlike Burr and Hamilton, who distinguished themselves in the Revolutionary war, Jefferson had no military experience. Yet he believed that conflict, even when it erupted into violence, was beneficial, even necessary for an enduring liberty, as he wrote in 1787, "The tree of liberty must be refreshed from time to time with the blood of patriots and tyrants. It is its natural manure."

The Treaty of Paris (1783), between Great Britain and the United States, which ended the revolutionary war, set the stage for western expansion. It recognized not only that the thirteen original states were independent and sovereign, it also set boundaries to American expansion: to the north Canada, to the South, Florida, then under Spanish dominion, and to the West, the Mississippi River. Burr, who did not continue as Vice-President for Jefferson's second term, having been abandoned by Jefferson and his party, hoped to make his fortune in this Western expansion, and he raised an army to achieve it, for his conscience was not bound by the Treaty of Paris, and he looked further west and south. He is said to have hoped to become emperor of Mexico. His adventures resulted in armed conflict. Article III, section 3 of the Constitution defines treason as armed conflict against any of the United States. Jefferson had him arrested and tried for Treason. He was acquitted.

The moral of this historical narrative is that one should not idealize, or worse, idolize the founders of this nation. They bear no halos. But what they achieved, represented and prescribed in our Constitution deserves respect seasoned with critical understanding, without which their achievement will not last.

Founding Sisters

THE FOUNDERS OF THIS NATION WERE MEN. However, if social practices had permitted, as they now do, there was no lack of women, of high intelligence, broad learning, and noble character, who could have filled the role of founder as well an any man, perhaps better, and there is reason to believe that some of them did so indirectly. Their contribution must not go unnoticed.

Chief among them is Abigail Adams (1744-1818). As the wife and mother of two presidents, she was well situated to be of influence, and her correspondence is proof that she did not hesitate to use it and that her correspondents took her seriously. Her correspondence with her husband reveals that he regarded her as his equal, and she was his confidant and advisor. They also demonstrate her thorough knowledge of the principles and practices of government. Other founders also sought her advice, and she was willing to give it. Thomas Jefferson valued it, or at least pretended to.

She was an early and outspoken advocate of women's rights, the education of women, and the abolition of slavery.

She was also a formidable correspondent, as Thomas Jefferson was to learn to his discomfort. After the Revolution, Adams and Jefferson had become estranged, moving in opposite directions politically. In 1800, Jefferson defeated Adams in the Presidential election and began to reverse many of the policies that Adams had initiated during his term as President, from 1797 to 1801. His goal was to dismantle Federalism. In 1804, during his first term, Jefferson's daughter died. Abigail wrote him a letter of condolence. She had known Mary Jefferson as a child and had been for a time her surrogate mother. They were devoted to each other. Abigail's letter was heartfelt. She concluded the letter by describing herself as someone "who once took pleasure in subscribing Herself your Friend".

Jefferson responded quickly. He expressed gratitude for her letter and for all the kindnesses she had shown to his daughter, and he expressed regret that he and John Adams had become estranged. He recalled how closely they worked for independence, and how, in spite of their political differences, they had always been respectful of each other's opinions and policies in spite of their differences. However, he recalled one occasion when it seemed to him Adams had betrayed their friendship. Towards the end of his term as President, Adams had appointed a number of men to Federal judgeships. Jefferson, who succeeded him, took this as a personal affront, for "they were among my most ardent political enemies, from who no faithful cooperation could ever be expected". Nevertheless, time and the remembrance of their former friendship and the warm sentiments of her letter, moved him now to forgive her husband. The tone of his letter is condescending.

Abigail Adams response was a powerful putdown. She wrote, with great irony, that she had considered Jefferson's sentiments "and have given them every weight they claim". But first, she wanted to set the facts straight. Adams's appointments were entirely within his right and were faithful to the Constitution. At the time he made the appointments, President Adams had no reason to believe that he would not be elected to a second term. The men whom he appointed were of high competence and of unquestioned loyalty to the Constitution and to the rule of law.

Above all, she was deeply offended by the manner in which Jefferson succeeded to the Presidency: "I have never felt any enmity towards you Sir for being elected President of the United States. But the instruments made use of, and the means which were practiced to effect a change, have my utter abhorrence and detestation, for they were the blackest calumny, and foulest falsehoods." She was referring to the slanderous remarks about her husband published by James Thomson Callender, a journalist of dubious reputation who enjoyed Jefferson's patronage and protection.

Jefferson responded, defending his actions, but to no avail. Two more letters would follow back and forth. The last, written by Abigail concluded that Jefferson had become an unprincipled defender of his political actions. This, she noted, was a judgment of reason. "Having once entertained for you a respect and esteem, founded upon the Character of an affectionate parent, a kind Master, a candid and benevolent Friend, I could not suffer different political opinions to obliterate them from my mind, and I felt the truth of the observation, that the Heart is long, very long in receiving the conviction forced upon it by reason. Affection still lingers in the Bosom, even after esteem has taken its flight." Jefferson did not respond.

Abigail Adams was only one of several founding sisters. Others were Elizabeth Schuyler Hamilton, Hamilton's Eliza; Lucy Flucker Knox, wife of Henry Knox, a leading revolutionary war general, and the two Theodosia Burrs, mother and daughter. All were highly cultivated, well read, decisive, and articulate.

Elizabeth Hamilton was a descendent of two distinguished New York families, the Schuylers and the Van Rensselaers, who were also very wealthy. Socially and economically, she married beneath her, but this was compensated by Hamilton's brilliance, energy, and ambition. In conversation, she was overshadowed by her sister Angelica, with whom Hamilton also formed an intimate relationship, although probably without impropriety. After his death, in 1804, she remained faithful to his memory. She died in 1854 at the age of 97.

Theodosia Burr the elder was also an early advocate of women's education. Twice widowed, she and Burr were attracted to each other perhaps more for each other's intelligence and learning than for their physical beauty, although neither were lacking in this respect. She introduced Burr to the writings of Mary Wollstonecraft, whose writings on the rights of women have become classics. Their first child, a daughter and the only one of their children to reach adulthood, was also named Theodosia. Both Theodosias were ahead of their time.

Theodosia the elder and Burr regarded themselves as partners in in life. Together they oversaw the education of their daughter, until the senior Theodosia's death in 1794 at age 47. Burr continued on his own. Theodosia the younger became fluent in Greek, Latin, and French, read the classics and could hold her own in philosophical and political conversation in the most learned company. The collegiality between Burr had his wife continued with his daughter. After his trial for treason and acquittal in 1807, Burr went into self-exile in England and she saw to his needs. He returned to the United States in 1812, after the outbreak of war with Great Britain. Theodosia, who had married and was living in South Carolina was on her way to meet him in New York. The ship on which she was sailing disappeared, she was lost at sea. She was 29. Burr was heartbroken. The loss was the nation's also.

DISCOVERING AMERICA

VICTOR NUOVO

ESTABLISHMENT

Mercy Otis Warren's America

AMONG THE FOUNDERS OF THIS NATION, one whose name is rarely mentioned except among scholars and specialists is Mercy Otis Warren (1728-1814). Yet she was held in the highest regard by prominent founders. Jefferson thought her a genius, Adams considered her "the most accomplished lady in America." A contemporary historian, deeply familiar with her work, described her as "one of the best writers in the English language of her generation, of either sex, on either side of the Atlantic" and compared her to the great English historian Edward Gibbon.

She was a prolific writer of plays, poems, political satires, and letters. Just after the Boston Tea Party, John Adams enlisted her literary talent in the struggle for independence. She began with a satire in a local newspaper entitled "The Squabble of the Sea Nymphs" in which she depicted the scattering of tea in the sea as an offering to Neptune, that he sanctioned after seeking the counsel of Sea Nymphs — Neptune remembered the Ladies. Thereafter she became one of the foremost literary advocates of "the common cause". The title of a recent biography describes her as "The Muse of the Revolution".

But the comparison to Gibbon is perhaps more apt. Warren's massive history of the American Revolution, published in 1805, invites comparison with Gibbon's *Decline and Fall of the Roman Empire*. The editor of a recent collection of her correspondence observes that even when writing a familiar letter, "she rarely wrote just a note," rather "she seemed to imagine history looking over her shoulder." She was, like Gibbon, a philosophical historian of very high caliber. (It should be noted, however, that she disapproved of Gibbon's work because of his low regard for Christianity, counting it as a major cause of Rome's imperial decline; nevertheless, she studied his book and was doubtless influenced by it.)

She wrote history as an unsentimental Deist and Christian moralist. She was also a political realist, who viewed the historical past as "a deposit of crimes", "the record of everything disgraceful or honorary to mankind" whose leading causes are "ambition and avarice" that "actuate the restless mind". "From these primary sources of corruption have arisen rapine and confusion, the depredation and ruin that have spread distress over the face of the earth from the days of Nimrod and Caesar" to the present.

One would expect from this that a mood of deep pessimism would pervade her writing. But Warren's view of America could be bright and hopeful. She envisioned this country as a land of opportunity. Her vision was Jeffersonian. Like her forbears, she perceived the land as "a vast variety of soil and climate" capable of producing "everything necessary for convenience and pleasure", a place where "everyman might be lord of his own acquisition". She envisioned a nation of "yeoman farmers" who were economically self-sufficient, educated, and politically free. And because the land was vast and ever expanding, the population would increase also, by a growing birth rate but also immeasurably by immigration, "Here it might rationally be expected, that beside the national increase, the emigration to a land of such fair promise of the blessings of plenty, liberty, and peace, to which the multitudes would probably resort, there would be exhibited in a few years, a population almost beyond the calculation of figures". I am reminded of the motto on the Statue of Liberty: "Give me your tired, your poor, Your huddled masses yearning to breathe free, The wretched refuse of your teeming shore. Send these, the homeless, tempest-tossed to me, I lift my lamp beside the golden door!"

But Warren was not so naïve as to believe that her vision could be easily realized. It depended for its realization on the virtue of its citizens, and she watched this diminish in public and private behavior, much as we do today. She perceived three dangers to our nation. First, a failure of national intelligence: the ideals of the revolution, so well expressed by Jefferson in the Declaration of Independence, were in danger of "dwindling into theory"; second, popular discontent, distrust and disillusionment with government, and a tendency towards anarchy; third, private ambition and the accumulation of wealth and power. One need only follow the news to become convinced that they remain present dangers, and that Warren's historical insight was prescient and deep.

What did she mean by "ideals dwindling into theory"? Warren was no anti-intellectual; quite the contrary. One need only take note of her learning, evident in all she wrote, to be clear on that. The expression signifies a disembodiment of once vivid ideals and their change into mere speculative hypotheses, opinions of punditry, rather than calls for action. It also signifies an ignoring of facts based on keen observation and experimentation. In these respects, she writes as an activist and a scientific empiricist. What could be more modern?

She was cognizant of popular discontent. She sympathized with the plight of poor farmers, many of whom were veterans of the Revolutionary Army, and took their grievances to heart; her sense of justice made her become their public advocate.

On the other hand, she suspected all private ambition and had a strong dislike for the rich and famous; she despised elitism, but she was ever a lover of truth and philosophically sophistication.

Politically, she allied herself with the party of Jefferson, variously named Republican or Democratic, or Democrat Republican. She was an anti-Federalist and opposed ratification of the Constitution and the form of government it created. She especially worried about the power given to the chief executive; and in general, she wanted more power retained by the states. She faulted the unamended constitution for its lack of an explicit declaration of rights. She labeled supporters of the Constitution "Monarchists", and singled out John Adams, her sometime friend and sponsor, as their leader. She was especially bothered by Adams' statement that the British Constitution made Great Britain a Republic. This difference ended their friendship. But Abigail Adams remained her friend and fellow advocate of "the Ladies".

Postscript: Warren's *History of the Rise, Progress, and Termination of the American Revolution* (1805) is available online, along with her poems and other writings, and also in a modern inexpensive paperback reprint. It should be required reading in our schools. I also recommend "The Squabble of the Sea Nymphs", which is available online, although it is filled with classical allusions, and one should at hand have a classical dictionary.

Thomas Jefferson

A GENERATION OR MORE AGO, composing an essay about Thomas Jefferson would have been an unproblematic task. It would begin with a description of a man of outstanding intelligence, limitless curiosity, and boundless energy, a scholar, a master of the English language, a patriot possessed by a deep passion for liberty, the author of the Declaration of Independence, a principal founder of our nation, a very great man of world historical importance, whose genius and accomplishments would be celebrated in this nation for as long as it endures.

With the passing of time, none of this has become untrue, but all of it has become problematic, ambiguous, and needful of numerous qualifications. What caused this change? No doubt some of the causes are in ourselves; the times have changed and because of these changes we interpret the past differently. But it may be that the passage of time and the accumulation of political experience have put us in a better position to judge the past. Historical enquiry is always in the last analysis objective and retrospective, a search for truth in this instance infused with moral urgency, because the past we have received determines what we are now.

In particular, Jefferson's opinions about race have come under closer scrutiny and these along with the fact that he owned slaves, some of whom he fathered, who were instrumental to his wealth and comfort, and this has led to skepticism about his character and the sincerity of his passion for liberty. This skepticism is not new. Abigail Adams, who had low regard for Jefferson, felt it and confided it in a letter to her husband. Her comment was cited in a previous essay, but is worth quoting again in full:

"I have sometimes been ready to think that the passion for Liberty cannot be Equally Strong in the Breasts of those who have been accustomed to deprive their fellow Creatures of theirs. Of this I am certain that it is not founded upon that generous and Christian principal of doing to others as we would that other should do unto us."

Jefferson's views on race are summarized by him in *Notes on the State of Virginia* (1787), which was written as a guide to the State of Virginia in the late eighteenth century, a report giving detailed accounts of its geography, geology, climate, flora and fauna, people, public works, religions, customs, government, and laws. It was written to fulfill a request of the secretary of the French Ambassador, who desired a better knowledge of the states. It is a descriptive work, dispassionate, factual, and comprehensive, requiring considerable research to complete. Jefferson began composing it in 1780 while he was governor of Virginia, the war of revolution was ongoing, and Virginia was a major theatre of war. It was written under great hardship and personal misfortunes — chief among them, the death of his wife. It is extraordinary in scope and detail. I suspect that no public official living today anywhere in the world could provide such a learned account of his country, written by himself without any assistance.

Shortly after independence, a committee of the Virginia legislature was created to revise state laws to fit their new political condition. Jefferson was one of its members. He summarized their recommendations in section XIV of *Notes*, which at the time of writing were not yet enacted. They cover a broad range of topics: property rights, citizenship, public works, taxes, and more. Notable among them is the recommendation for religious freedom "on the broadest bottom".

He mentions another statute to be added as an amendment that would emancipate all slaves "born after the passing of the act". Note this did not apply to those already existing under the conditions of slavery. They remained "movable property", like tools and furniture, only their children born after the enactment of these newly revised laws would be free; they would remain under their parents' care until they reached adulthood.

When they became mature adults these free-born blacks would be deported, or rather "colonized" to another continent, after being provided with the means to live gainful lives in their new homes — arms, household implements, domestic animals, etc. Jefferson recognized the economic costs of this policy. Slaves did essential work and would have to be replaced. White workers would have to be imported to replace them. All this would require additional expenditures. It would be far less costly to incorporate American-born free Blacks.

So, Jefferson asks, "Why not retain and incorporate the blacks into the state?" Why not allow them to remain as free citizens?

He gives two sorts of answers, one social or political, the other biological. Socially, he thinks it would be impractical, because of "deep rooted prejudices entertained by the whites; ten thousand recollections by the blacks of the injuries they have sustained". He imagines that their presence will result in an enduring conflict between fueled by white prejudice and black resentment. It is the latter that he emphasizes. Jefferson never enquired about the causes of white prejudice.

He supposed that these social consequences arise from racial distinctions that "nature has made". Among them is color: "whether the black of the negro resides in the reticular membrane ... whether it proceeds from the color of the blood", or of the bile or from other physical sources, whatever its cause, it is a physical condition that can't be changed, and, Jefferson opines, it has moral and aesthetic consequences. White faces are supposed to be more diverse in color and therefore more expressive, the emotions and passions are visible, in contrast to the "immovable veil of black which covers all the emotions of the other race". He adds other differences which he has observed that he also ascribes to nature. Blacks are more ardent, but less reflective, "in memory they are equal to whites; in reason much inferior, as I think one of them could scarcely be found capable of tracing and comprehending the investigations of Euclid; and that in imagination they are dull, tasteless, and anomalous".

It is disheartening to read all this, and difficult to write about it. Yet it is part of the American heritage, and considering it enables one to understand why the Declaration of Independence has become ambiguous to us. One can also hope that the memory of it can become a potent antidote to white prejudice, which is still a vital contagion — it inhabits the White House*.

*This essay was originally published June 13, 2019.

George Washingon

NO NARRATIVE OF THE FOUNDING OF THIS NATION is complete that doesn't take account of George Washington. Yet of all the founders, he is the most difficult to represent. As the historian Joseph Ellis has written, the trouble with Washington as a subject of history is that it is hard to find the man beneath the monument, which was being erected over him even while he was still living. In his most recent book, *American Dialogue*, Ellis sums up the historical problem succinctly: "There was a man named George Washington who walked the earth during the last two-thirds of the eighteenth century, but he has been transformed into an otherworldly demigod whose wisdom is silence"; and he concludes this with this remark: "There are no words on the Washington Monument." Perhaps this is why accounts of the nation's founding, focus on Adams, Hamilton, Jefferson and Madison as agents who promoted the main outlines of the American Republic while assigning Washington the passive role of presiding demigod.

But in fact, not only did Washington have a well-considered idea of what this nation should become, but as the first President, he, perhaps more than any other, set it on its course, so much so that it can be said that, for better or for worse, much of what the United States has become is what he intended and worked for. What did he intend?

He intended that the United States of America should become a great continental power, continuing on its western expansion, and that, in this course of development, white Protestant Englishmen would displace the indigenous nations that had been settled here for millennia. He acknowledged that the land was originally theirs by right, and insisted that their displacement should be accomplished only through legal means: through purchase or through treaties carefully executed and faithfully observed, for he acknowledged that the indigenous peoples had constituted themselves into sovereign nations each with its own body of law and system of government, and that they deserved proper respect in keeping with the law of nations — the very idea of international law was relatively new, invented in Holland by Hugo Grotius during the previous century in his influential work, *The Right of War and Peace*. It served as a guide to the European settlers to North America.

Washington also foresaw that, as European settlers acquired more and more of the land and developed it for agriculture, an activity that he engaged in on a grand scale, thereby greatly enriching himself, the economic prospects of these indigenous peoples would decline with the loss of hunting grounds and the diminishment of wildlife. The remnant of native peoples would continue to live in their much diminished territories, and to survive they would have to change their mode of life and take up agriculture or animal husbandry and become acculturated to a European mode of life. This policy is best described as economic genocide, enforced by brutal acts of savagery.

When contemplating the European settlement of America and the western expansion, it is important to ask, "Who were the savages?" But I digress.

The dominant theme of the Farewell Address is the union of the states under the federal constitution. Washington depicts the union of states under one government, thereby making it one nation, as "the Palladium of [the people's] political safety and prosperity," endowing it with a religious, albeit nonsectarian quality. "Palladium" refers to Pallas Athena, the mother goddess of Athens, whose enormous statue presided over the citadel of classical Athens. The more perfect union brought about under the new Constitution, included a national name "American," and a new identity for every citizen — a cultural identity "you have the same Religion, Manners, Habits and political Principles" and a "common cause. The benefits that would derive from this union were not only political but also economic, for this new nation would not only increase in territory and fertile land also rich in resources, but in access to the sea; hence, it would become a leader in world commerce. Washington envisioned The United States as what it has become: an international economic powerhouse.

Washington's Farewell Address was his valedictory. It included a defense of what he hoped would become his legacy, for it was under his direction that in accordance with the Constitution that the organization and practices of the federal government first took shape. He acknowledged that the government he celebrated was a government of the people and that its chief purpose was, in accordance with the Constitution, "to secure the blessing of liberty" for all the people, now and hereafter. But he was emphatic that in the enjoyment of liberty the people must make this government and its law a standard for all their future actions. "This government, the offspring of our own choice uninfluenced and unawed

… completely free in its principles, in the distribution of its powers, uniting security with energy, and containing within itself a provision for its own amendment, has a just claim to your confidence and your support. Respect for its authority, compliance with its Laws, acquiescence in its measures, are duties enjoined by the fundamental maxims of true liberty." Or again, "The very idea of the power and the right of the People to establish government presumes the duty of every Individual to obey the establishment of Government."

Washington's Address was not greeted with universal applause, hence another prominent theme in the Address was a warning against factions and party politics. What he warned against was already a reality. Jefferson regarded the Address as a Federalist tract, and he was not wrong. When he became president in 1800, Jefferson went about dismantling Federalist policies and institutions. But in his second term, he found it necessary to restore much of what he dismantled.

It has been noted that Washington did not write the Farewell Address by himself. He had two noteworthy collaborators: James Madison and Alexander Hamilton. In 1792, near the conclusion of his first presidential term, he planned to retire and had asked Madison to draft a valedictory. Circumstances brought a change of mind, and he served a second term. In 1796 he was firm in this decision. He had retained Madison's draft, which became the first part of the Address, and he drafted a second part. He gave these to Hamilton to complete.

To suppose that the final product did not contain Washington's thoughts and purposes would be a mistake. His genius was as an organizer and leader in war and peace. His achievements were extraordinary just because his modest sense of himself enabled him to rely on the exceptional talents of others to fulfill his own purposes. The Farewell Address is an expression of Washington's administrative genius. He was the American Pericles.

The Farewell Address ended with a caution to avoid special relations or alliances with other nations. "Against the insidious wiles of foreign influence, the jealousy of a free people ought to be constantly awake." "The Great rule of conduct for us, in regard to foreign Nations is in extending our commercial relations to have with them as little political connection as possible." One of his legacies, for good or ill, is American nationalism.

Postscript: Read Washington's Farewell Address for yourself online at: avalon.law.yale.edu/18th_century/washing.asp.

Benjamin Franklin

THE PRINCIPAL FOUNDERS OF THIS NATION played different but complementary roles in its creation. Adams was its chief theoretician; Jefferson and Hamilton, no less knowing, excelled at putting theory into practice, although moving in contrary ways; Washington as chief executive made it actual.

What of Benjamin Franklin? He played many roles: drafting the Declaration of Independence, concluding a peace with Great Britain, framing the Constitution, and securing a prominent place for the United States among the international community of nations, and more, much more: he was this new nation's presiding genius, which is a fitting role for a philosopher.

It is often overlooked that even before his eminence among the founders Franklin had gained international reputation as a philosopher. David Hume (1711–1776), who is arguably the most eminent British philosopher of the 18th Century, in a personal letter to him recollecting his visit to Edinburgh in 1762 wrote this: "America has sent us many good things: gold, silver, sugar, tobacco, indigo, etc.; but you are the first philosopher and indeed the first great man of letters, for whom we are beholden to her." Franklin excelled at "natural philosophy" and gained international reputation for his investigations into the nature of electricity; a product of this inquiry is the lightening rod, which he invented. He also invented the Franklin stove, bifocal glasses, and the urinary catheter, all of which are evidence of his study and insight into the workings of nature. In the early modern period in Europe (the 17th and 18th centuries) philosophers did more than deal with abstractions.

To promote such studies, he helped found the American Philosophical Society and the University of Pennsylvania. He was elected a member of the Royal Society of London and was awarded honorary degrees by the University of Edinburgh, and by Harvard and Yale, which commissioned a portrait of him that still hangs in its library.

What sort of philosophy did Franklin profess? It was motivated by an insatiable curiosity that knew no limits and could be satisfied only by free enquiry and free expression. It was also public and therefore practical, often concluding with some practical benefit; and it was non-dogmatic. At its root was a profound moral seriousness and a preoccupation with human conduct.

Overall, Franklin's stance is skeptical. Thus, while his research into the nature of electricity were constructive and important, he never seems to have pursued a more general inquiry into the nature of things, into what was then known among philosophers as speculative physics or metaphysics. In this respect, he is much like his friend David Hume. He did not believe that humans, in spite of their intelligence, are so well situated, or so penetrating in their insight to gain a knowledge of the fundamental laws by which nature operates, how it originated and what its end might be.

Franklin was a professed theist, and he repeatedly expressed belief in a universal providence, believing that a wise and universal intelligence governed the course of events in nature and history. He had little use for religious dogma, which he considered doubtful and morally repugnant; as a youth he repudiated the strict Calvinism in which he was nurtured. He doubted the divinity of Christ, but admired Jesus' moral teaching. He valued religion because it was for many the only secure way to be sufficiently motivated to sustain a morally upright life. Yet he had only mockery for those who supposed that their good behavior and good works were a source of divine pleasure, as though God should require such things and still be God, all-wise and in need of nothing.

His writings were devoted almost entirely to practical morality, and they led to his fame and fortune. This all began almost by chance, and as the result an ingenious deception. While still a youth — he was 16 — he submitted a letter to the editor of a local newspaper which was owned and managed by his older brother James to whom he was apprenticed as a printer. The letter was rejected. He then invented a fictitious persona, "Silence Dogood," a middle-aged widow, and submitted letters over her name, slipping them under the door of the press room. They were printed. They contained practical reflections on everyday life in the colonies and on the human comedy generally and they excelled in homespun wisdom.

In 1733, he published *Poor Richard's Almanack* under the pseudonym Richard Saunders and followed it by a new edition every year for a quarter century. It made him rich. An almanac is a book of useful knowledge, containing a calendar, astronomical and astrological information, household information, and everyday practical wisdom. It was a fitting work for a philosopher of Franklin's bent to write, a skeptic, one who knows only that we are creatures of time, cast adrift in a changing and therefore uncertain world, and who must every day take our bearings anew and recognize the challenges we face, which differ with the changing seasons and situations in life. Philosophically, Franklin the philosopher might be described as an existentialist, but of a purely American kind, uninfected by the narcissism and romanticism of his later European counterparts.

The most enduring part of Franklin's almanacs are his moral teachings, which consist not of general rules or abstractions, but of apothegms, which are concrete, specific, observations of character that contain implicit rules of behavior; they are universal in meaning and soul searching in intent. There is no adequate way to describe them, for each has its own idiom. I conclude this essay with some examples:

"The heart of a fool is in his mouth, but the
mouth of a wise man is in his heart";

"Humility makes men twice honorable";

"Full of courtesie, full of craft";

"Most of the learning in use, is of no great Use";

"Hunger is the best Pickle";

"Pride is as loud a Beggar as Want, and a great deal more saucy";

"If you would be revenged of your enemy, govern yourself";

"Would you live with ease, Do what you ought, and not what you please";

"Without justice, courage is weak";

"A rich rogue is like a fat hog, who never does good 'til dead as a log";

"He that lies down with Dogs, shall rise up with fleas";

"Kings [Presidents] and Bears often worry their keepers."

Postscript: The main virtue of maxims is their apparent self-evidence, they foster belief without thinking. However, in promoting this sort of homespun morality, one wonders whether in this respect Franklin might be considered as a founder of American anti-intellectualism, unintended by him, but perhaps inevitable, for the maxim is the ancestor of the soundbite, which has become a staple of our culture.

Adams and Jefferson in Retrospect

On July 4, 1826—50 years after the signing of the Declaration of Independence—at 6:30 in the evening, John Adams died. His last words were "Thomas Jefferson still lives." He was mistaken, for Jefferson had died four hours before. That both men should have died on the same day, and on that particular day seemed remarkable to many then as it does now. Given the narrative of American independence and nation-building, it was a fitting conclusion; to many it was providential, proof that the founding of this nation was not a mere historical accident. It is also remarkable that 17 years before the event, a mutual friend, Dr. Benjamin Rush (1746–1813) had a premonition of it in a dream, which he described to John Adams in a letter dated October 17, 1809; he wondered whether the dream might be prophetic. Rush was a signer of the Declaration and a noted physician who did pioneering research into the physical causes of psychological disorders. He had taken on the task of restoring the friendship between Adams and Jefferson.

Once close friends and co-revolutionists, Adams and Jefferson had become political enemies. Profound differences about the nature of government and of domestic and foreign policy, exacerbated by their opposing views on the French revolution, created feelings of resentment and estrangement between them that in their retirement only deepened. Rush worried over this; it was not good for them or for the nation. He wrote to both men and, having secured from them mutual expressions of continuing respect and love, informed each of what the other had written, urging them to renew their friendship. Finally, on the first of January 1812, Adams wrote Jefferson a short note wishing him "many happy new years," expressing his long and sincere esteem, and signing off as "your faithful friend." Jefferson quickly responded with expressions of "sincere esteem" and pledged his "unchanged affections and respect." After a hiatus of eight years in their friendship and correspondence, which followed Jefferson's unhappy exchange with Abigail Adams, they resumed their correspondence, which continued until the year they both died.

What is most impressive about these letters is their humanity. Adams and Jefferson had grown old and were acutely aware of their declining powers and loss of physical agility. At the outset, Adams was 77, Jefferson 70; when the last letters were exchanged in 1816, Adams was 90, and Jefferson 83. The founders of this nation were not Titans or great heroes, but mortal human beings, frail, afflicted with infirmities, and haunted by regrets. Their letters are a fitting postscript to the founding, bringing it down to earth.

Here were two old men, sensitive to their age. In his first letter, Jefferson excuses himself for his "senile garrulity," to which Adams, always the Latinist, responded that he has retaliated with "my Senectutal Garrulity." But they were also founders of a new nation, whose destiny to expand across a continent and become a world power was already becoming evident. Prominent in its founding, they had served in the highest offices of its government and shaped its policies. These were prodigious achievements, and they took pride in them. Yet they did not glory in them or try to relive them. Jefferson allowed that he would be ready to live them over just as they happened, but Adams demurred, mostly recalling the pain and regret. When, in 1825, Jefferson congratulated him on his son's succession to the Presidency after a distinguished career as a diplomat, his response was subdued.

Jefferson writes about his poor health and the difficulty of keeping physically active. He commends Adams on his continuing good health and describes his efforts: he rides every day but adds that he is able to walk only a mile. Later he would tell of having imbibed the waters at Warm Springs and the ill effects that resulted from it which seemed to cause a rebellion in his body that never relented. It was the onset of Uremia or kidney disease, which eventually caused his death. Adams was more robust, walking three or four miles "every fair day." But he complains of the onset of tremors, and the palsy, which makes writing difficult for him. Both rejoice in their families, notwithstanding the pain of the early death of children, delighting in their grandchildren, and Jefferson of a great-grandchild.

Jefferson was still active, not as a politician but as an educator, overseeing the University of Virginia, which he had founded, still shaping its curriculum, and building up its faculty, but increasingly spending his days in his library at Monticello searching for ancient and modern wisdom. "I have given up newspapers in exchange for Tacitus and Thucydides, for Newton and Euclid, and I find myself the much happier." Adams was far more pessimistic. Although he was continuously gathering books, most of which he would never read, "100,000 would not be enough," he was harsh in his criticism of what he found in them. He applauds his friend's activity only so far as he studies Newton and "the contemplation of the heavens". He had had his fill of ancient learning and its purported wisdom and of politicians to boot: "I am weary of Philosophers, Theologians, Politicians, and Historians. They are immense masses of absurdities, vices, and lies." He preferred journeymen and the products of their honest labor.

And yet, he continued to collect books, and continued to read them. It is a curious paradox, but not unusual.

They contemplated death. Commenting on Samuel Johnson's fear of death, Adams wrote mockingly, "a friend of Johnson told me that Johnson died in Agonies and Horror of Annihilation … Dread of Annihilation! Dread of Nothing? A dread of Nothing should be no dread at all. Can there be any real substantial rational fear of nothing?" Adams expressed no fear of death: If it is annihilation then, that he will remember nothing of it: if he survives, he will exist under the same rule of the universe that he did in life. In his old age, Adams, once a Christian, seems to have become a philosophical naturalist. His God is evident only in the natural order of things: a great intelligence, but indifferent to the sorrows and misfortunes of his creatures. "That there is an active principle of power in the Universe is apparent, but in what substance that active principle of power resides is past our investigation. The faculties of our understanding are not adequate to penetrate the Universe". He has only harsh words for the biblical account of creation which reduced the universe to "this little ball" of earth: and proceeded to "spit upon it".

Both men expressed anxiety about the future of the nation, although both expected it would become a great world power. They continued to affirm liberty and equality as the fundamental principles of society; they expressed scorn for monarchies and aristocracies, worried over the growing wealth-based aristocracy in this nation, opposed slavery, and cultivated a serious interest in the culture of the indigenous American nations.

Postscript: The institution of slavery and the treatment of the Indian nations make it difficult to write a celebratory history of the United States. The great divide in wealth increases the difficulty.

Growing A Divided Nation

BETWEEN THE YEARS OF 1783 AND 1848 the United States realized its greatest territorial expansion. The Treaty of Paris (1783) formally ended the war for independence. It determined that the territory of The United States of America extended westward to the Mississippi River. In 1803, during the presidency of Thomas Jefferson, this boundary was moved westward by the Louisiana Purchase. In 1819, Spain ceded Florida to the United States. In 1846, The Oregon Territory was acquired through negotiation with Great Britain, and in 1848, in the Treaty of Guadalupe-Hidalgo, which concluded the Mexican War, Mexico ceded large territories to the United States, extending the territory of the nation "from sea to shining sea."

Thus, by mid-century the consolidation of the lower 48 states was nearly complete. To finish the story: in 1853 the United States purchased a strip of land from Mexico that now forms the southernmost parts of Arizona and New Mexico; Alaska was purchased from Russia in 1867 and became a state in 1959; Hawaii was acquired (or seized) and made a territory in 1900, and a state in 1959.

In 1823, the Monroe Doctrine became official U.S. policy. It gave warning to European nations that the United States would regard any more colonization by them in the Western hemisphere as "dangerous to its peace and safety". This ended the era of European colonization in this hemisphere and the United States emerged as its paramount power.

The European powers would have to go elsewhere to grow their empires, which they did. Colonialism flourished accompanied by racism, gross injustice, and a growing threat of world war. Nothing really changed.

As the nation grew, it became more and more divided. Two issues divided it: slavery and states' rights. The Constitution had established one nation under one supreme law enhanced by a bill of rights, but its benefits accrued mostly to white males, for they alone were enfranchised. Sectional differences persisted — economic, moral and ideological. The right of states to ignore or nullify federal statutes was asserted. There was talk of secession. The future of the union was in doubt.

In a speech delivered to the Senate in 1850, Daniel Webster accurately described the state of the nation: "It is not to be denied that we live in the midst of strong agitations and are surrounded by very considerable dangers to our institutions and our government. The imprisoned winds are let loose. The East, the North, and the stormy South combine to throw the whole sea into commotion, to toss its billows to the skies, and disclose its profoundest depths."

Webster desired calm. The question before the Senate was whether to enact legislation establishing the mandatory return of fugitive slaves. Webster, who represented Massachusetts, where slavery was illegal, nevertheless was speaking in favor of what would become the Fugitive Slave Act of 1850.

With regard to slavery, Webster was a pragmatist. He opposed slavery in principle and expected its eventual abolition, but he accepted the fact that slavery was legal in many southern states; he believed that the Constitution protected it. His stance regarding current laws (at the time) in slave states was that the institutions of slavery in those states must be respected.

It should be noted that a part of Article 4, section 2 of the Constitution—repealed in 1865 and replaced by the 13th amendment—required that persons in servitude in one state who escape to another state or territory be returned to their masters. It prohibited any state from providing them sanctuary. Webster, among others, interpreted this to apply to fugitive slaves. The Fugitive Slave Act was supposed to implement this constitutional provision.

Webster was convinced of the rightness of his position. He was a public official, a senator, soon to become Secretary of State, and he regarded it as his constitutional duty to uphold the Constitution and the laws of the United States, even those whose essential morality he might find doubtful. Public officials, when carrying out their duties, were supposed to respect the law, and no other principle, which is not to say that Webster was unprincipled. His stance is a perfect instance of *stare decisis* (see *Postscript*). This put him in conflict with the Abolitionist Movement and its founder, William Lloyd Garrison (1805–79).

As a youth, Garrison favored the abolition of slavery. Initially, he supported a policy of gradual emancipation, and he joined the American Colonization Society, an organization founded in 1817, to facilitate the return of freed slaves to Africa. This led to the creation of the African state of Liberia. President James Monroe gave his strong support; hence the name of the capital of Liberia, Monrovia.

By 1830, Garrison concluded that this position was morally wrong, that the only proper course of action was immediate emancipation and enfranchisement of all slaves followed by their integration into American society: freedom and equality. He founded a newspaper, The Liberator, which became the leading voice of Abolitionism in this country. In the first issue he declared his editorial policy: The practice of slavery is a moral wrong of such magnitude that the only way to deal with it is to end it immediately. In his advocacy he promised to be "as harsh as truth, and as uncompromising as justice".

Webster respected the abolitionists and believed them sincere, but he worried that their practices were extreme and impractical. They were moral absolutists for whom "everything is absolutely right or absolutely wrong", hence there was no ground for compromise.

Abolitionists failed to recognize that there were many on the other side, Webster maintained, "religious men, with consciences as tender as any of their brethren in the North, who do not see the unlawfulness of slavery," and others who "whatsoever they may think of it in its origin, yet take things as they are, and, finding slavery to be an established relation of the society in which they live" fail to see a way end it. He based his argument on the premise that there are good people on both sides of the question.

He feared most of all that a divided nation would be left without a peaceful way to settle its disputes and heal its divisions, that the bond of union would be broken, that secession and war would become inevitable. His worries were prophetic.

However, Webster failed to mention that the government in which he held office never actively entertained the possibility of ending slavery. He mentions the need for compromise, but never says how that should be spelled out. In the end, this eloquent cheerleader of the nation was paralyzed by his fears, and when facing the devil, he lost his nerve.

Postscript: *"Stare decisis"* literally means "Stand by what has been decided", which in a judicial context signifies a respect for precedent.

The Political Thought of John C. Calhoun

IN STUDYING THE HISTORY OF AMERICAN POLITICS from 1826 to the Civil War in search of persons who shaped it, I find that there are two who deserve special notice and warrant a place in this series: Andrew Jackson (1767–1845) and John C. Calhoun (1782–1850). Jackson led the nation "through force of personality," rather than through his intellect. Calhoun excelled in intellect and was arguably the most eminent American political philosopher of the first half of the 19th century, as well as a most influential member of Congress, a statesman and distinguished public servant. He was also a creator of the politics and culture of the old South, and, as senator for South Carolina, a defender of slavery and staunch protector of Southern interests against what he came to regard as the ever-growing aggressive power of the North, which surpassed the South in wealth and population. He epitomized the politics and culture of the old South.

Calhoun was born in South Carolina on March 18, 1782; he received little formal education, just enough to enable him to enter Yale College as a junior in 1802. He graduated with a B.A. in 1804 and continued his studies at Litchfield Law School, in Connecticut. He was admitted to the Bar in 1807 and practiced law for a while. In 1810, he was elected to the House of Representatives by his home district and served until 1817, when he was appointed Secretary of War by President James Monroe; he served for eight years. From 1825 until 1832 he served as Vice President under two presidents: John Quincy Adams and Andrew Jackson. He resigned the office in 1832 to run for the U.S. Senate representing South Carolina; he was elected and served until his death in 1850.

Calhoun wrote two books on politics, *A Disquisition of Government* and *A Discourse on the American Constitution*, but he chose not to publish them. They were published posthumously, in 1853. The latter is a commentary on the Constitution, the former presents a complete theory of government. It has become a classic. In scope and intelligence, it belongs in the same class with Hobbes' *Leviathan* and Locke's *Second Treatise of Government*.

To acquire a proper understanding such works requires that one approach them in two ways: first, by viewing them against the background of the long tradition of European political thought; second, by setting them in the context of their immediate political situation. Both are necessary. If the latter is ignored, then the ideas they present become floating abstractions, sublime perhaps but of no immediate relevance, mere objects of contemplation to be stored in the mind for future use; if the former, they are reduced to political slogans that do little more than incite the emotions, lacking insight, and intelligence — this often goes by the name of popular thought. An interpretation that is complete, rich, and ennobling, and yet also practical must treat both together: context and tradition. Calhoun's *Disquisition* is very short, but this was possible only because he was able to draw upon tradition, which allowed him to be brief but also comprehensive.

He begins with the observation that all human animals are social beings and are inclined by nature and circumstance to live with others in society. Necessity motivates them, for they cannot hope to survive without the assistance of others. They are also incited by feelings of sympathy for others; of empathy and a desire to unite with them. They soon learn that many more benefits accrue to them only by joining together: society becomes the seedbed for human creativity, for the forward movement of civilization, for fulfillment, and even transcendence: the arts and sciences are its products, along with domestic tranquility.

Yet, individual feelings of sympathy for others are counteracted by a far stronger personal self-interest, which leads to conflict between the members of a society; suspicions and resentments increase among them and often lead to violence unless unchecked. To counteract this tendency, force and law, the instruments of government, are necessary to maintain order and create peace. Thus, we find that all human beings seek to live together in society, but a stable society requires the force of law.

Yet, no matter how forceful the power of government, it will not easily accomplish its purposes unless some means be found to moderate a volatile society, means that are both just and effective. Only a sense of unanimity will achieve this. Here, Calhoun provides his most ingenious and constructive proposal. This is his idea of a concurrent majority.

As Madison and Hamilton warned, in every political society factions are inevitable, because of the manifold interests of the people, these may be ideological, regional, social, economic, religious, even philosophical. Everyone is a partisan for something, and the deep and inherent motive for self-preservation only exacerbates differences, and the people divine into rival parties, each promoting its own interest at the expense of all others. Majority rule is no solution; from the situation of the minority, it is just another form of tyranny. What is needed is unanimity.

Calhoun would have us imagine a government made up of representatives of all the parties existing in society, each party representing some particular constituency or special interest. In legislating or enacting some government policy every party would have a veto. Deliberation must be ongoing, a constant activity, aiming at a common good, until through a long series of compromise, unanimity or concurrence were achieved. It is government by majority rule, but not the rule of a numerical majority but of a "concurrent majority," by policies in which each party concurs, or at least agrees not to exercise its veto, which is concurrence in the lowest degree, like when a chief executive chooses not to exercise the veto, but nevertheless allows a bill to become law without her signature.

Calhoun admits that this would be a very slow process of government. In this respect, he seems to have anticipated the very idea of slow democracy.

It is easy to see how Calhoun's idea of government by concurrent majority could be used by him to negotiate on behalf of southern interests, to compensate the fact that the South was becoming more and more a minority region. It should also be noted, however, that Calhoun was also a staunch unionist, and although his activity became increasingly regional, he never abandoned his loyalty to the nation; he wanted both. And it is just possible, if his idea of a concurrent majority had been taken seriously, and practiced by all, that slavery might have been abolished sooner by a far less violent process. But this is only conjecture.

Postscript: There are echoes of Hobbes in Calhoun's political thought, and a slighter echo of Locke but he departs from both by ignoring the idea of a social contract. Perhaps this was intentional for implicit in the idea of a social contract is the rule that government must be by consent of free and equal persons, which in the old South included only white males; Blacks did not count as persons.

The Age of Jackson

ANDREW JACKSON (1767-1845) WAS PRESIDENT of the United States for two terms, from 1829 until 1837. He also ran for the office in 1824 and received the most votes, but he didn't receive a sufficient majority in the electoral college to elect him outright. It remained for the House of Representatives to decide the winner, and they chose John Quincy Adams, who had run second. Henry Clay was then Speaker of the House, and it was rumored that he and Adams had made a deal. Shortly after he took office, President Adams appointed Clay Secretary of State and the rumor was confirmed, at least in the minds of Jackson supporters. They cried foul and loudly condemned what they perceived to be a "corrupt compromise." Thus the campaign was launched that would elect Jackson president in 1828. In the meantime, his supporters employed every political means to sabotage the administration of John Quincy Adams. It was the beginning of partisan politics as we know it.

Jackson's presidency is regarded by some leading historians as a transformative moment in the history of the nation. He was the first president who did not belong to the eastern elite. His victory marked the demise of the New England based Federalist Party and the triumph of the Democratic Party, the party of Jefferson. But Democrats had abandoned Jefferson's vision. He envisioned a nation of small farms, an agrarian society, self-sufficient, whose primary government consisted of local councils, a participatory democracy, a counterweight to, if not a substitute for, the growing central government. The vision was no longer practical, even Jefferson had abandoned it. Democrats recast themselves as the party of ordinary people, farmers and workers, who were the real economic base of American society, although they possessed little of its wealth, and whose voice was not heard. Jackson became their president. His administration brought many major changes: social, economic, and cultural, which together caused a fundamental change in the character of the nation. Commerce became the national vocation and by it the nation greatly increased its wealth and power and standing among the nations.

The historian Arthur Schlesinger, Jr. credited Jackson with this achievement and named his history of the period "The Age of Jackson." He depicted him as the first "populist president." But this judgment has not gone unchallenged. For one thing, the label does not seem to fit the man, who was more of an aristocrat than an ordinary citizen, as the historian Richard Hofstadter has noted, he was a member of the Southwestern aristocracy, whose way of life combined characteristics of "frontier roughnecks" and "landed gentry," interested primarily in gambling, horse-racing, and hard drinking, whose behavior was "lawless, individualistic, quick-tempered, and brawling," but also "courtly, sentimental, unreflective, and touchy." He greatly valued his honor and fought a duel to defend it; he was wounded in the faceoff, a bullet lodged close to his heart and could never be removed — though grievously wounded, he remained steady, took careful aim, and killed his opponent. He migrated west to Tennessee, where he practiced law, became moderately wealthy, purchased land, acquired slaves, and became politically well-connected. He headed the local militia; subsequently he became a national hero at the decisive battle of New Orleans, all of which opened a pathway to the presidency.

But, the question remains, just what did Jackson do that warrants calling him "the People's President" and naming an era of American history after him. Unlike, John and John Quincy Adams, Jefferson, and Madison, Jackson, does not seem to have had a well-worked out political vision. He was not reflective, not a man of ideas, which seems to have become the norm for American presidents. There is nothing in his papers that would suggest otherwise. His inaugural addresses are prosaic and uninspired; they are balanced policy statements. If he was motivated by a passion, it is evident only in his actions. As a soldier, he had distinguished himself by his courage, daring, and savagery, and no doubt these characteristics carried over in his presidency.

One episode during his presidency supports these contentions—the so-called Bank War. It concerned the Second Bank of the United States, which was chartered by Congress in 1816, the charter expired in 1836. In 1829, Jackson expressed doubts about its constitutionality. The Bank was not a government agency, but a private corporation that nevertheless operated much like a national institution with unrestricted powers. Its purpose was to facilitate industrial and commercial growth, to provide credit and to regulate currency. The United States government provided 20 percent of its assets. Its original design was conceived by Alexander Hamilton. As a congressionally chartered national institution, it was not subject to state laws or regulation; it could not be taxed by them. In opposing the Bank, Jackson went to war against the eastern moneyed establishments, the power elites, who were its principal beneficiaries, and he won. In 1832 Congress passed legislation to renew the charter of the Bank for another twenty years. In a conciliatory gesture, they proposed a few reforms. Jackson vetoed the bill, because he believed it to be "subversive of the rights of the States, and dangerous to the liberties of the people" by giving too much power to the rich. His veto was sustained, and no subsequent legislative effort was made to renew it. Its charter expired in 1836.

Jackson was also victorious against the efforts of John C. Calhoun to promote states rights over the interests of the national government. Calhoun, who was then vice-president, defended the right of states to nullify federal laws when the laws required them to act against their own self-interest. Jackson's response was swift and decisive, and constitutionally astute. He noted that the Constitution did not form a league of states, but a government of the people, that is, of all the people individually and not as members of states, a single nation that cannot be divided. One is reminded of Lincoln's speech the launched the Lincoln/Douglas debates: "a house divided against itself cannot stand."

One last outcome of Jackson's administration must be mentioned. This was the Indian Removal Act, which caused the relocation of Indian peoples from their ancestral lands east of the Mississippi to territories farther west. He described the policy as benevolent, a happy consummation. He concluded his message to Congress with these remarks, justifying the act of removal:

> "And is it supposed that the wandering savage has a stronger attachment to his home than the settled, civilized Christian? Is it more afflicting to him to leave the graves of his fathers than it is to our brothers and children? Rightly considered, the policy of

> the General Government toward the red
> man is not only liberal, but generous. He
> is unwilling to submit to the laws of the
> States and mingle with their population.
> To save him from this alternative, or
> perhaps utter annihilation, the General
> Government kindly offers him a new home,
> and proposes to pay the whole expense of
> his removal and settlement."

In fairness to Jackson, the great genocidal wrong of this policy was not his alone, but the nation's. It is still ours.

Establishing the Rule of Law

THE CONSTITUTION OF THE UNITED STATES provides for three branches of government, each exercising a separate power: legislative, executive, and judicial. Legislative power is the power to create laws; executive, the power to carry them out. Judicial power is the power of judgment. The term is derived from the Latin word "judex," a judge, a public official who decides what is right, equitable, or good, in accordance with fundamental law.

Article III of the Constitution provides that "the judicial power of the United States shall be vested in one supreme Court, and in such inferior Courts as the Congress may from time to time establish." It also provides that, unlike officials of the legislative and executive branches who serve for limited terms, federal judges shall serve without limit of tenure on condition only of good behavior. Writing in the *Federalist Papers*, Alexander Hamilton explained that a life appointment would make the justices independent and immune from the pressures of partisan conflict and special interests.

A similar case has been made for academic tenure, which is intended to free scholars from intimidation or recrimination in their searches after truth. He saw no danger in these life appointments, for the Supreme Court is the least powerful branch of government: it has "neither FORCE nor WILL, but merely JUDGMENT." Hamilton may have been too optimistic. Life tenure on the bench or in the academy, may be a necessary condition for impartiality, but it is not a sufficient one. The person who has this privilege must also have the will to achieve it.

In 1789, Congress passed a Judiciary Act, which determined that the Supreme Court should consist of a chief justice and five associate justices. It also created two levels of inferior federal courts: district courts and circuit courts of appeal. The system is basically the same today — although the number of associate justices has increased as has the number of district and circuit courts. The Judiciary Act of 1789 also clarified the scope of powers of the Supreme Court. Among other things it determined that it should be the appeals court for cases decided in federal circuit courts, and that it had the authority to issue "writs of mandamus," that is, to issue commands or directives to officials in the executive branch of government to perform certain actions.

For over a decade after its creation, the Supreme Court was overshadowed by the other branches of government and by national events. This changed, when, on Feb. 24, 1803, the court issued its decision on the case of Marbury vs. Madison.

The decision was written by the fourth Chief Justice, John Marshall (1755–1835). Marshall had been appointed Chief Justice by John Adams, during the final year of his administration, having served as Adams' Secretary of State. He was Chief Justice from Feb. 4, 1801, until July 6, 1835, when he died. He remains the longest-serving occupant of that office, and is generally acknowledged that no one did more to establish the rule of law than he, and that the decision concerning Marbury vs. Madison was a pivotal moment not only in the history of the court but also of the nation.

During the final lame duck year of his presidency, John Adams made a number of other judicial appointments, among them, the appointment of William Marbury as justice of the peace for the District of Columbia. These appointments enraged Thomas Jefferson, for it meant that when he assumed office, he would have to contend with a large contingent of Federalist judges, among them persons he considered his worst political enemies.

There was no denying that the appointments were valid. Adams had sought and received the requisite advice and consent of the Senate. The appointment documents were properly drafted and signed, and the presidential seal was affixed to them. They were sent to the office of the Secretary of State for delivery to the designated appointees. This happened the day before Adams left office. However, the documents were never delivered by the outgoing Secretary of State, who was also John Marshall. When Jefferson took office, their existence became known, and the new President directed James Madison, the new Secretary of State, not to deliver them. He supposed that this would nullify the appointments.

Marbury disagreed. He appealed to the Supreme Court, asserting his right to the appointment and demanding that he receive it; the appointment document was legally enacted; it was his warrant to office; and he had a right to it. The court heard his appeal. Madison, who as Secretary of State was defendant, made no appearance, nor did anyone from his office appear to defend him. It was no doubt a calculated snub. Nevertheless, the Court proceeded and issued a decision that was in Marbury's favor, although it must not have satisfied him.

First, it was decided that Marbury's appointment was valid. The fact that it was not delivered did not nullify it. But if the appointment was valid, then Marbury had a right to it and to the office to which it entitled him. Second, it was determined that there must exist a legal remedy to satisfy Marbury's right. Here Marshall, in writing the decision, appealed to the common law principle *ubi jus, ibi remedium* (wherever there is a right, there is a remedy). What sort of remedy? A judicial command, or *mandamus*, directing the Secretary of State to deliver the appointment.

In summary, the court argued that Marbury's appointment was valid, and therefore he had a right to receive it; and that since he had a right, there must exists a judicial remedy to satisfy it. So far, so good. It is from this point on, however, that, from Marbury's standpoint, things went awry.

In section 13 the Judiciary Act of 1789, power was granted to the Supreme Court to issue "writs of mandamus," that is, judicial commands or directives, and that this power was under its original jurisdiction. On the basis of this article, the legal remedy that Marbury desired seemed to reside in the Supreme Court, for on the basis of this statute, the court could have provided the remedy that Marbury desired. However, it did otherwise. The court declared Section 13 of the Judiciary Act unconstitutional. In doing so, it did not deny Marbury a legal remedy, but not this one. Marbury retained the right to appeal to a lower court. He chose not to do this.

Although this might seem an unhappy ending, most legal scholars would disagree, for by its action, the Supreme Court claimed a power not before asserted, for it is not written in the Constitution, the power of judicial review, or the power to decide what the law is. Section 13 of the Judiciary Act was repugnant to Marshall and his colleagues because, by enacting it Congress extended the scope of the Court's power beyond limits set by the Constitution. Congress had violated the Supreme Law of the Land. In the Court's decision, Marshall asserted that the Constitution is that supreme law, and that in accordance with this law, the Court is empowered to judge all other statutes and to decide their status under the Constitution.

Much has been written about this decision and the motives of Marshall, its author. Were they merely political? Marshall was a Federalist. Although related to Jefferson, a second cousin, he disliked and distrusted him. The feeling was mutual. Had the court issued a writ of mandamus, there is no doubt that Jefferson would have ordered Madison to ignore it. Instead, Marshall chose a path that Jefferson was unable to block, and by doing so, he secured a power peculiar to the judicial branch.

VICTOR NUOVO

TRANSCENDENTALISM

Transcendentalism

"TRANSCENDENTALISM" SIGNIFIES THE FLOWERING of culture in New England during the first half of the 19th Century when it threw off the burden of Calvinism, indeed of all institutional religion — even Unitarianism was felt to be too limiting. Among its leading figures were Ralph Waldo Emerson, Henry David Thoreau, and Margaret Fuller, who will be featured in this series, and there was a host of others. It was a powerful cultural movement; its influence has been broad and deep; it has persisted to the present day, so that reading about it will often involve a measure of self-discovery, and a longing to be as they were.

But Transcendentalism was not a homegrown product. It roots were in European literature and philosophy. Transcendentalists admired and borrowed from the English Romantic poets Wordsworth and Coleridge. But they were even more indebted to European philosophers. One can trace their genealogy from Renè Descartes to Immanuel Kant and forward to G. W. F. Hegel.

Kant was the first to employ the term philosophically. He used it to describe knowledge that does not derive from things external to us, like fields and fountains and flowery meadows, or from the many familiar objects that surround us, but a knowledge we must already possess in order to know anything at all. In the opening section of his great work, *Critique of Pure Reason*, Kant wrote that although our knowledge begins with experience, not all of it derives from experience, rather there are certain things we know before we can ever know anything. The aim of transcendental philosophy is to discover this knowledge that is prior to all other knowing. Accordingly, Kant embarked on a search for what he called the à priori presuppositions of two other sorts of knowledge: knowledge the external world and knowledge of our moral duty. The place where the search for this prior knowledge takes place is in ourselves, in our consciousness, and it involved an ascent to ever higher levels of selfhood, or self-transcendence.

The outcome of the first enquiry was disappointing. Kant concluded that we will never come to a perfect knowledge of the external world and of external things. We are not able ever to know them as they are in themselves, but only as they appear to consciousness, only as they affect us, mere appearances. This led him on a kind of archaeological search of human consciousness. And after much labor of self-examination, he discovered a system of general categories or rules rooted in the mind that frame its perceptions of the external world. He concluded that this was the prior knowledge he sought.

Of course, appearances are not illusions, and through hypothesis, experiment, and analysis we can learn very much about the nature of things so far as they relate to us. And we can experience the infinite expanse of nature and its sublime beauty. But underlying all of this, there is also a knowledge of general concepts that we use to make sense of what we see, and hear, and touch: the idea of a thing, of one or many, and composite things, of processes, of change and causation, of reality and illusion, of yes and no and a host of logical distinctions. He called them categories or rules of consciousness; by employing them, we are able to understand the universe that surrounds us and in which we have our being.

The search for knowledge of our moral duty discloses something far more sublime; we discover our moral selves, our being as persons, through which we have access to a higher world, one that is governed by a higher moral law. This ascent to a higher law is the goal of transcendentalism.

Here is Kant's summary of his discoveries:

"Two things fill the mind with ever new and increasing admiration and reverence, the more often and more steadily one reflects on them: the starry heavens above me and the moral law within me. I do not need to search for them and merely conjecture them as though they were veiled in obscurity or in the transcendent region beyond my horizon; I see them before me and connect them immediately with the consciousness of my existence. The first begins from the place I occupy in the external world of sense and extends the connection in which I stand into an unbounded magnitude with worlds upon worlds and systems of systems, and moreover into the unbounded times of their periodic motion, their beginning and their duration. The second begins from my invisible self, my personality, and presents me in a world which has true infinity but which can be discovered only by the understanding, and I cognize that my connection with that world (and thereby with all those visible worlds as well) is not merely contingent, as in the first case, but universal and necessary. The first view of a countless multitude of worlds annihilates, as it were, my importance as an animal creature, which after it has been for a short time provided with vital force (one knows not how) must give back to the planet (a mere speck in the universe) the matter from which it came. The second, on the contrary, infinitely raises my worth as an intelligence by my personality, in which the moral law reveals to me a life independent of animality and even of the whole sensible world, at least

> so far as this may be inferred from the
> purposive determination of my existence
> by this law, a determination not restricted
> to the conditions and boundaries of this
> life but reaching into the infinite."

Transcendentalists seized upon these words; the words became for them a confession of faith, a creed. Emerson may have memorized them; for I am repeatedly reminded of them as I read his writings.

What has all this to do with political thought? Very much. A Transcendentalist regards every human person as a moral being, a free agent guided by reason, a person capable of self-knowledge and limitless self-transcendence. Anyone who knows this cannot be a slave or enslave anyone else. Freedom and equality for all is the only conclusion one can draw from this; and thus the blessings of liberty may be secured for all.

Postscript: Kant wrote three *Critiques,* the first concerning the knowledge of external things, and the second concerning moral knowledge, *Critique of Practical Reason;* the third, *Critique of Judgment*, concerns judgments of value, especially aesthetic values, the beautiful and the sublime.

VICTOR NUOVO

A Platonic Digression

AFTER REVIEWING THE PREVIOUS ESSAY, I realized that my account of the philosophical background of American Transcendentalism was incomplete. Its historical roots reach back in history well before Kant, to Greek antiquity. If we can believe Plato, Socrates was the first transcendental philosopher, and on his own account, he was taught by a woman, Diotima, a prophetess from the Greek city of Mantinea. To learn about this, one must read Plato's *Symposium*. This will not be an unpleasant digression. Indeed, I can think of no other book, past or present, that is more delightful, inspiring, transforming, transfiguring.

"Symposium" is a Greek noun; it denotes a banquet that usually ended in a drinking contest. Plato's *Symposium* depicts a gathering of aristocratic men during a holiday festival. They had feasted the day before and were hung over. One of the group, Eryximachus, a physician, remarks that excess drinking is harmful and suggests an alternative: an evening of discourse; each member of the party shall deliver a speech honoring Eros, the god of love, who of all the gods is the most neglected and yet the most worthy of our affection. This was agreed. The remainder of the *Symposium* consists of six speeches celebrating Love. Socrates is the last to speak and most of the remainder of this essay will be a summary of what he said.

This is not to say that the other speeches are not worth reading. They are all delightful. One in particular, by Aristophanes, is especially memorable. He begins with a narrative of the first human beings; they had spherical bodies, two heads, four arms, and four legs — bodies well suited for acrobatics and somersaulting and looking in both directions, which facilitated their movement. Some of them were male, others female, and still others androgynous. They were a haughty race, and the gods, offended by their pride and arrogance, and tiring of their insolence, punished them by slicing them in two; each half was left with one head, which the gods turned around, so that they would thereafter look down on their shame; and they were made to fear that if they did not learn humility, the gods would repeat the process. Aristophanes describes love as the longing for one's other half, for wholeness; the object of that sexual desire depends on whether one's original state was male, female, or binary. Commentators on the *Symposium*, have observed the irony of this speech. Aristophanes was a famed comic playwright, and his speech, although comic, reveals a serious passion deep in the recesses of the soul. Of course, his speech is a product of the art of Plato.

Socrates' speech is a narrative of what he learned from the prophetess Diotima. He tells how she began by cross-examining him in a manner reminiscent of Socratic questioning. The outcome was to convince Socrates that Eros, or Love, was not a god. But neither was he a mere mortal. Rather, Love is something in between, a *daimon* or spirit, dwelling in the soul, the cause of all desire, longing, and aspiration. To be spiritual is to be possessed, driven by a longing for something that transcends physical pleasure; it is to be in a state of being between mortality and immortality, a mortal longing for what is immortal, eternal, and for what is truly noble and good, for source of all value. Spirit resides in every human soul, and it is most manifest in engendering, giving birth, bringing forth new life with which comes expectation and hope. Socrates learns that pregnancy is not a condition of a one gender only; it inhabits both. Without it there would be no human creativity.

Diotima tells Socrates that every human being is pregnant "in body and soul: and on reaching a certain age our nature yearns to beget." The conjunction of man and woman is a begetting for both. It is a divine affair, this engendering and bringing to birth, an immortal element in the creature that is mortal. It is beauty that drives this yearning, this passion to beget. Beauty "presides over birth as Fate and Midwife; and when the pregnant approaches the beautiful it is endowed with grace and gladness, and the soul overflows in begetting and bringing forth." It cohabits with the beautiful and gives birth.

Diotima remarks that the human soul, unlike the divine, is driven by desire to give birth, because it is mortal, because only by engendering another life does life continue — she suggests that animals feel this too. But to accomplish this, the mind must transcend its mere mortal vision of physical things to encounter beauty itself, pure, unalloyed, and infinitely productive; and not only this, but also what is good, radiant, and of infinite promise. This transcending of the mind is not a flight into abstraction, away from mere sense, from what we see and feel and touch, from all that is concrete. What she imagined to be the eternal form of beauty was rich and full and fulfilling, encompassing the fairest, the finest, and the noblest of things. No artist can be without this vision, which is beauty "existing by itself, in singleness of form, eternally itself," for it is the fountain of all creativity, in art and much more.

Plato gives this idea of the beautiful and the good a novel political turn. Love is the desire to engender something that is not only beautiful to the senses, but also noble and good, which is elevating to the mind; something that will overcome the deficiencies and uncertainties of the human condition. And this is best exemplified in the creation of a civil society, and of the institutions of government, and its laws. This alone is sufficient to free us from the limitations and infirmities of our frail human nature.

Now a civil society flourishes only if its members are virtuous. Our worst deficiencies arise not from our mortality, but from our immorality, from meanness of spirit, selfishness, envy, willfulness, and willful ignorance. To overcome this, we must transcend ourselves, and it is only by this means we become truly social beings, ever engendering more noble laws, ever refining our institutions ensuring that are accommodating to all, and above all just. To be a citizen is to be a participant in an ongoing creation and celebration of life.

Postscript: Everyone should read Plato's *Symposium*. It is very readable and there are many good translations of Plato's *Symposium*. Consult your local bookseller.

Margaret Fuller

MARGARET FULLER (1810-1850) WAS BORN Cambridge, Mass.; she was a prominent member of the Transcendentalist Club. In her short life she produced a remarkable body of writing: literary, philosophical and journalistic. She was homeschooled by her father, who early recognized her genius. She read Latin by the age of six, and by her teens was well read in the Latin Classics. She also became fluent in Greek, French, German and Italian. This was not an altogether happy time for her. Looking back on it, she wrote, "I had no natural childhood."

She was from a young age self-reliant. The early death of her father left her, the eldest of seven siblings, head of the family, which she supported by writing, teaching and editing; she became editor of *The Dial*, the Transcendentalist journal. She was also a political activist. As foreign correspondent for the *New York Tribune*, she traveled to Italy in 1848 to report on the struggle for Italian unity and soon joined it. There she met a young revolutionary, Giovanni Ossoli, with whom she bore a son. When the revolution failed, they decided to return to the United States; they married and began their journey, and had almost reached their destination when they were shipwrecked and lost off the coast of Long Island. Only the body of their son was found. A memorial in Cambridge has this tribute: "Margaret Fuller. By birth a child of New England; by adoption a citizen of Rome; by genius belonging to the world." It is apt.

Her major work, *"Woman in the Nineteenth Century,"* grew out of an essay, originally published in *The Dial*. The essay bore the title, "The Great Lawsuit, Man versus Men, Woman versus Women." Her book is frequently described as an early feminist work. But this is too limiting; she was concerned just as much about men as about women, which she makes very clear at the outset. "By Man I mean both man and woman: these are the two halves of one thought ... twin exponents of a divine thought." The essay and the book might be read as an enlightened exposition of Genesis 1:27: "So God created man in his own *image*, in the image of God created he him; *male and female created he them.*" The image of God to which "Man" conforms is androgynous, which is the theme of her whole work; its central thesis is that in order to become truly human, men and women must transcend their birth gender or "cisgender" (to use a current term) and embrace the other, indeed they must embrace the whole of human nature in all its diversity.

In the light of its thesis and the arguments presented in it, *"Woman in the Nineteenth Century"* should be read by all; it is a philosophical work—a sophisticated discourse on human nature and destiny in which male and female are two complementary parts of a whole. It is also a counsel of human perfection.

But in 1844, perfection had not yet come to America—we still await its coming. Up until then, history and politics had been all about men, more specifically, about white men; and even though human equality was espoused as "a golden certainty," the "monstrous display of slave-dealing and slave-keeping" continued; nor did women possess the right to vote, or any other active rights of citizens. These gross deficiencies in American democracy had to be overcome if this nation were to realize its destiny. This is the theme of "the great lawsuit." Fuller perceived an essential connection between the practice of slavery and the demeaning of women. Both were rooted in a denial of human equality. Hence just as the abolitionist assumes "that one cannot by right hold another in bondage, so should the friend of woman assume that a man cannot by right lay even well-meant restrictions on a woman. If the negro be a soul, if the woman be a soul, appareled in flesh, they are accountable only to one Master [God]. There is but one law for all souls."

The central theme of her work is the union of male and female, as two necessary parts of one whole. Historically, this union is marriage, but she sees it as more than an institution.

She dismisses the Biblical narrative of Adam and Eve, for it demeans the role of the woman. She is depicted as a mere helper, not as a partner or complement. And in the narrative of the Fall, she observes that Adam excuses himself for his disobedience by blaming it all on Eve.

Fuller perceives four kinds of marriage that are not ideal, but well-tried conventions. The first is a "household partnership." "The man furnishes the House; the woman regulates it. Their relation at best is one of mutual esteem, mutual dependence. Their talk is of business, their affection shows itself by practical kindness."

The relation is good as far as it goes, but the desire for wholeness seeks more. Hence the next two. First is a relation of "mutual idolatry," a marriage rooted in romantic love, which she regards as too narrow for human fulfillment. The second is more fulfilling: "intellectual companionship, which she also describes as a marriage of friendship. But she holds out for an even higher relationship, which she characterizes as religious, by which means "a thirst for the true and the good, not the love of sect and dogma," a bond whose principle is transcendence, whose goal is human fulfillment, of wholeness.

Postscript: "*Woman in the Nineteenth Century*" is not an easy book to read. Fuller does not state a thesis and defend it with arguments. Rather she uses historical anecdote and literary analysis designed to take possession her readers' minds and transport them to truth. She worried that her book required "too much culture" to be easily understood. But it is eminently worth reading, and the diligent reader will reap a rich reward. There is a paperback edition of her book, published by Dover Books. It may also be found in "*The Portable Margaret Fuller*" (Viking), which includes a selection of her other writing, including an autobiographical sketch.

Ralph Waldo Emerson

READING EMERSON MAY BE COMPARED TO TAKING a shower. Instead of streams of water falling gently and pleasantly over one's body, there is a steady flow of words that infuse the mind and cleanse it of the grime and mire of the vulgar world, of common opinions and fashionable novelties and their grinding effects. His words elevate the mind to a consideration of nobler, purer things; they awaken in the conscience a longing for perfection; they induce in consciousness a sense of infinite possibility. They are not meant as a means to escape the world, but to cause a higher engagement with it.

There is, I believe, in all Emerson's writing a constant purpose, which is self discovery; but this should not be taken as selfishness, rather it prescribes the conquest of every selfish motive. The self that he sought and represented in his writings is not that of the narcissist or the resentful misanthrope, not the creature of Twitter and Facebook and the so-called social media. It discovers itself in the contemplation of nature; it is not a mere subject, but a "superject"—a term invented by the philosopher Alfred North Whitehead to signify the integral relation of subject and object, of self and world.

"If a man would be alone, let him look at the stars. … One might think the atmosphere was made with this design, to give man, in the heavenly bodies, the perpetual presence of the sublime." "I become a transparent eye-ball; I am nothing; I see all; the currents of the Universal Being circulate through me; I am a part or particle of God." So wrote Emerson in his earliest major publication, *Nature* His God is not the person of biblical tradition, but nature itself as a never-ceasing benevolence.

Similarly, in an address to the senior class of Harvard Divinity School he said this:

> "In this refulgent summer, it has been a
> luxury to draw the breath of life. The grass

grows, the buds burst, the meadow is spotted with fire and gold in the tint of flowers. The air is full of birds, and sweet with the breath of pine, the balm-of-Gilead, and the new hay. Night brings no gloom to the heart with its welcome shade. Through the transparent darkness the stars pour their almost spiritual rays. Man under them seems a young child, and his huge globe a toy. The cool night bathes the world as with a river, and prepares his eyes again for the crimson dawn. The mystery of nature was never displayed more happily."

This "poetic naturalism" is recurrent in everything he wrote. And there is perhaps no better way to educate students in a lasting love of nature than to have them read Emerson.

But always there follows a higher theme. The sentiment of nature opens the mind to a higher moral self. "A more secret, sweet, and overpowering beauty appears to man when his heart is opened to the sentiment of virtue. ... he learns that his being is without boundary; that, to the good, to the perfect, he is born, low as he now lies in evil and weakness." This higher self perceives the essential goodness of everything. "Evil is merely privative, not absolute: it is like cold, which is the privation of heat. ... Benevolence is absolute and real. So much benevolence a man has, so much life hath he."

This moral sentiment is the expression of true religion, rising above the artificial bonds of every tradition, free from meaningless ritual and sectarian feelings. It is its own revelation and so requires no other justification. Yet, it is always new. It encompasses everything, and it excludes no one from its obligation to do no harm, only good. Hence, it is the only proper basis of civil society, for only a civil society whose citizens are free from the fetters of every particular identity and chauvinism can long endure.

It may be objected that this conclusion is far from self-evident. It is not the reason that most nations, perhaps any at all, would give to justify their existence, let alone recognize the need for it. Yet I am inclined to believe that the moral self that Emerson imagines in his writing, a self that strives to encompass all of nature in a benevolent embrace, and that owns its own identity by means of a sense of moral obligation to others is a sure prescription for a nation's abiding health.

For consider our current political situation. The United States is plagued by two crises, one political, the other global.

First, the political crisis. In 2016, the people of the United States (granted a minority of them) elected as president of the United States a person who is morally unfit for the office, or for any political office. A malevolent egoist, a pure narcissist, selfish and resentful. The crisis for thoughtful Americans was how to respond to this situation. The only antidote was to fill he moral void he created with their own moral decency. To resist evil with good. This crisis hasn't ended. The people of the United States, which is us, must practice overcoming evil with good. This is our only antidote to the present evil, our only sure means of resistance.

The global crisis is environmental. There is no doubt that our material way of life is leading us on a path of global extinction, not to mention that it is also a cause of increasing inequality and injustice, of pain and sorrow among many who are altogether innocent of the misuse of nature's resources by the rich and advantaged. The evidence is decisive, and to deny it is pathological. The encompassing embrace of nature that Emerson the poetic naturalist proposes promises a way not to save nature, for in the end, nature will take care of itself—and us as well—but a way of restoring us to a proper relation to the only source of our being and induce a proper respect for it. It might be said, "The fear of Nature is the beginning of wisdom."

Emerson on Experience

Ralph Waldo Emerson's earliest writings, on which the previous essay was based, portray a mind infused with a sunny confidence. In his later works his mood darkens; moments of doubt and uncertainty cloud his vision. This emergent mood is given somber and poignant expression in the essay "Experience." Emerson does not say what caused this change of mood. He mentions the recent death of son Waldo from scarlet fever. He was only five, an innocent child, and Emerson dearly loved him. Yet it would be a mistake to interpret this essay merely as a personal expression of grief; for his thoughts carried him beyond his grief to a broader vision of the human condition and the meaning of existence. It is somber, but not without hope.

The essay opens with a question. "Where do we find ourselves?" to which Emerson responds. "In a series of which we do not know the extremes, and believe that it has none." He imagines himself as having awakened into a dreamlike state, standing midway on a flight of stairs that appears to float in infinite space; its top and bottom extend out of sight. He has no idea of how he came to be there. His very being seems to be without substance and purpose, a mere sequence of conscious events without meaning or purpose. If there is any order to them, it is not one designed to accommodate us.

"Ghostlike we glide through nature, and should not know our place again. Did our birth fall in some fit of indigence and frugality in Nature, that she was so sparing of her fire … and though we have health and reason, yet we have no superfluity of spirit for new creation? We have enough to live and bring the year about, but not an ounce to impart or invest … We are like millers on the lower levels of a stream, when the factories above them have exhausted the water." "Dream delivers us to dream, and there is no end to illusion. Life is a train of moods, like a string of beads, and as we pass through them, they prove to be many-colored lenses which paint the world their own hue, and each shows only what lies in its focus." We have only experience to guide us.

The terms "experience" and "experiment" were once synonymous. They have the same Latin root: *experiri,* to be put to the test, to be made trial of — but to what purpose? Emerson imagines a human life as a series of trials, whose purpose is never revealed. Self-consciousness is an awakening to this condition, whose chief condition is disorientation. It is as though Nature has betrayed him.

Whereas as in "Nature" we find Emerson the transcendental idealist, in "Experience" he has become an existential philosopher. The former is an optimist. The latter inclines towards pessimism. To the former, the course of nature and history is managed and directed by an all-powerful, benevolent, wise spirit, whose purposes are evident to every inquiring mind and certain to be accomplished. Its values are objective and clear. The latter is caught up in a network of subjectivity that bars the way to truth, and efforts to escape it inevitably fail. Our state is prison of desperation. "There are moods in which we court suffering, in the hope that here at least, we shall find reality, sharp peaks and edges of truth. But it turns out to be scene-painting and counterfeit. The only thing grief has taught me, is to know how shallow it is." Even our feelings are diminished and deprived.

The idealist is well connected to the world, confident of its purposes. The existentialist is plagued by chronic neurasthenia. Writing of the death of his son, he despairs that "it does not touch me: some thing which I fancied was a part of me, which could not be torn away without tearing me, nor enlarged without enriching me, fall off from me, and leaves no scar." "I grieve that grief can teach me nothing, nor carry me one step into real nature." "Nothing is left us now but death."

Illusion, loss of feeling, despair, death, of being cast into the world for no purpose, without any end but oblivion. These are the themes of an existentialist philosopher, a skeptic and a pessimist. These are themes that better fit the world as it now is than as it appeared to be in New England 200 years ago. Perhaps after all, nothing ever changes. Life, the universe, everything seems to be governed by chance and necessity, with no ultimate purpose.

Notwithstanding, Emerson is undaunted. But the path that is now before him leading to a recovery of confidence and hope is not an easy one to follow; it is arduous, but it leads to wisdom. I'm reminded of the wise words of Sakini, in *Teahouse of the August Moon*. "Pain make man think. Thought make man wise. Wisdom make life endurable." Emerson would agree. Human nature is not devoid of resources that make it possible to endure life's many disappointments, and the capacity to endure them, and to employ them even creatively, in ways not before imagined.

Experience causes reflection; reflection, wisdom; and wisdom provides us with the strength to continue life's journey with modest optimism that fits the reality of things. The words with which he concludes this essay are worth remembering: Life goes on, "but in the solitude to which every man is always returning, he has a sanity and revelations, which in the passage of time he will carry with him. Never mind the ridicule (of Naysayers), never mind the defeat (of fortune): up again old heart!——it seems to say—there is victory yet for justice; and the true romance which the world exists to realize, will be the transformation of genius into practical power." And so the trial of life continues.

Thoreau at Walden Pond

AMERICAN CIVILIZATION WOULD BE MUCH diminished if Henry David Thoreau (1817-62) had not gone to live "alone, in the woods," by the shore of Walden Pond, for two years, two months and two days, in a house built by himself, subsisting on simple fare: fish, wild fruits and beans and other vegetables grown in a garden that he planted and tended.

He did not go simply to be alone. Thoreau was a writer and he wanted to be in a quiet place to finish writing a book. The book he completed was *A Week on the Concord and Merrimack Rivers*. But his experiences there provided the substance of a second book, *Walden*. Like his contemporary, Walt Whitman (1819–92), he wrote about himself, because, he confessed, there was nothing else that he knew better to write about than about himself and his experiences.

One must be clear, Thoreau was not motivated by any inflated sense of his own importance, or by the vain belief that others would want to read his story — which is the cause of too many books written today and too much talk clogging the airwaves. There is not the slightest strain of narcissism in his writing, and readers of *A Week* or *Walden* quickly discover that they contain much more than an account of the solitary adventures of Henry David Thoreau. Both books, indeed all his writings, are profound discourses about existence. And he felt the need to write.

One might ask, why did he feel this need to write? But what makes anyone a writer? I don't know. But I believe that writing is more than a vocation that one can take or leave; it is rather like a compulsion, and like other irresistible impulses that we all know, it yields feelings of great satisfaction and fulfillment and joy. Besides, the will to write is not an unimportant impulse, for without written words we would have no lasting civilization to speak of — no record of having lived that future ages might decipher and understand and learn from. The ages would have no meaning or perspective, and life no purpose.

Thoreau draws an interesting distinction between the spoken and the written word, between the orator and the writer. The orator "yields to the inspiration of the moment, and speaks to the mob," but the writer, undistracted by crowds, "speaks to the intellect and heart of mankind, to all in any age who can understand him." In this respect, the so-called social media, Facebook and Twitter and suchlike, are not writing, rather they should be classed with oratory, bombast or dribble, mere talk. The theme of "Walden" is civilization, and it is addressed to the ages.

The significance of the day when he began to live at Walden Pond, July 4, 1845, has been generally noted. It has been supposed that Thoreau chose this day to assert his independence as an individual against that of the nation. Thoreau dismissed this. He attached little if any importance to symbols and even less to himself. For him, the Fourth of July was just another day and he, just another individual dwelling in the land. Yet, intentional or not, the thought is illuminating.

Thoreau went to Walden Pond in search of truth, of a higher law transcending his mere existence or that of the nation. He went in the belief that this law would provide meaning and substance to himself and to the nation. This higher law had been the principle on which the nation had been founded, promising freedom and equality and justice for all. Yet, soon after its founding, the nation lost sight of this principle, if indeed it ever had it clearly in view — for from its beginning our nation sold its birthright to the cruel practices of slavery, as it now has to the vulgarities of commercialism and consumerism and fashion. He believed that the remedy for these ills existed only in will of the virtue of the citizen, for only by this could a nation be restored, and only citizens, acting as free persons, could possess it. Civic virtue is not a property that we inherit at birth, it must be clarified and understood and reasserted.

It was for these purposes, which are in essence political, that Thoreau went to live along at Walden Pond and practiced the profession of a writer.

But, first things first! Human existence is grounded in nature and depends upon it for its sustenance. Just "as the willow stands near the water and sends out its roots in that direction," so it is incumbent on human beings to rediscover their essential needs, and sources meet them, and having discovered them, to practice using them prudently, respectfully, and never wastefully. The longest chapter of *Walden* is devoted to economy, and one is reminded of a former campaign slogan, "It's the economy, Stupid." Thoreau's notion of the economy is very different and more basic than the latter, which was shallow and wrong-headed in any case. We are, after all, like all other plants and animals, creatures of nature, and we must concern ourselves above all with what we need to subsist and to try to secure them. Instead, we follow fashion, rather than necessity. Our manner of life is in all respects *à la mode*, whether it pertain to food, clothing, shelter, means of conveyance or entertainment. Thoreau went to live at Walden Pond to rid himself of fashion, which was flourishing all about him.

He went there for an even higher purpose, to discover what Immanuel Kant described as his "invisible self," his personality, his moral identity, which only reveals itself to anyone when the trappings of fashion have fallen away, when it stands unadorned before us. So, he carried with him not only household things, but armed himself with books and paper and pencils. And he wrote in the voice of that moral self:

"I do not propose an ode to dejection, but to brag as lustily as chanticleer in the morning, standing on his roost, if only to wake my neighbors up."

"A written word is the choicest of relics. It is something at once more intimate with us and more universal than any other work of art. It is nearest to life itself."

Civil Disobedience

HENRY DAVID THOREAU'S *CIVIL DISOBEDIENCE* rightly belongs among the founding documents of this nation. It complements the *Declaration of Independence*. It adds something altogether new to political thought, and therefore should be counted as a world classic.

In the first instance, like the *Declaration*, it was a declaration of independence, as fundamental in its resolution and its consequences as its predecessor. In 1776, the American colonies declared their independence from Great Britain, and thereby they became sovereign independent states. In 1846, one citizen, Henry David Thoreau, asserted the right of individuals to engage in acts of resistance against their government for reasons of conscience. He justified this action by appealing to a higher law, one that is purely just, which required his obedience even if it should cause him to rebel against the authority of his government and to disobey its laws.

Thoreau's act of civil disobedience consisted in his refusal to pay his taxes, which was required by law. Yet he claimed to have right on his side, "the right to refuse allegiance to and resist the government, when its tyranny or its inefficiency are great and unendurable."

He had two grievances against the United States government. One was its war with Mexico (1846–48), which he judged to be an act of aggression and territorial expansion by the government. The other was the institution of slavery, which it condoned. They were connected, for the territorial expansion that occasioned the Mexican War caused an increase in the number of slave-holding states and growth of the slave-economy in the nation.

Certainly the government's sanction of slavery and its imperialist expansionist policies were morally wrong, and they wrecked much havoc, against Mexico, against African slaves, and against indigenous people, whose lands were seized and who were likewise enslaved. It should be noted that the President whose policies he condemned and whose government he renounced was James Polk, a protégé of

Andrew Jackson, a nationalist, an imperialist, and slave holder, who is also greatly admired by the current occupant of the White House.

I will have more to say about Polk and the Mexican War in future essays. My present concern is with the very idea of civil disobedience, which it occasioned. I should begin by pointing out that Thoreau did not use this term, but the idea is his, which is all that matters. He preferred to write about resistance and rebellion.

To begin with, it is customary in accounts of political theory to distinguish between three types of government according to the number of those who govern: one, few, or many, hence: monarchy, oligarchy, and democracy. The founders of this nation, who prided themselves in having successfully rebelled against the tyranny of Great Britain and desiring to create a free and independent nation, believed that of these three forms of government, democracy is the best, because it is most inclusive, and that in this respect democracy is the end or goal of political progress.

Yet they worried that the principle of majority rule, by which democracies operate, could become a cause of tyranny; "the tyranny of the majority." Thoreau shared this worry. He concluded that the progress towards a more perfect government was not complete until the individual as such became supreme. "The progress from an absolute to a limited monarchy, from a limited monarchy to a democracy, is a progress toward a true respect for the individual." Hence, "there will never be a really free and enlightened State, until the State comes to recognize the individual as a higher and independent power, from which all its power and authority are derived, and treats him accordingly."

He then offers a vision of what is to come if a "free and enlightened state" were to be realized. He imagines "a State at last which can afford to be just to all men, and to treat the individual with respect as a neighbor; which even would not think it inconsistent with its own purpose, if a few were to live aloof from it, not meddling with it, nor embraced by it, who fulfilled all the duties of neighbors and fellow-men. A State which bore this kind of fruit [the fruit of difference and dissent] and suffered it to drop off as fast as it ripened would prepare the way for a still more perfect and glorious State, which also I have imagined, but not yet anywhere seen." Thoreau wrote "all men," where, to be consistent, he should have written "all persons" of whatever gender or sexual preference, and ethnicity. We must make these changes, for it brings purity to his idea.

What was it to be like, this "more perfect and glorious State"? Thoreau wrote that he imagined it, but believed it never "anywhere seen." It is a state that exceeds the promise of democracy, where everyone votes, but only the majority rules. It is a state in which the voice of every individual, if it is rational and just and not merely hateful, is never silenced; a society of persons enlightened by truth and justice, who regard each other with kindness and neighborliness and affection, one that is truly open in every way. Is it ever to be realized?

Thoreau's answer would have been "Yes and No." He imagined perfection as a goal that requires an infinitude of time to achieve, a goal that through our moral effort becomes nearer and nearer but is never perfectly realized, one that mathematicians would say is approached asymptotically. It is a political vision true to transcendentalist principles, and I'm inclined to believe, one that is true, if people can join together and work for it in harmony.

Thoreau believed moral perfection is achieved not by the individual alone, but by individuals in society, hence it is political perfection as well. The will to achieve it is a political will, to infinite progress, guided by principles of liberty, equality, enlightenment, neighborliness, and kindness, planted in a soil fertilized by dissent. It is a noble vision deserving of an Amen.

Postscript: In some collections of Thoreau's writing, the work *Civil Disobedience* is given an alternative title, *Resistance to Civil Government.* Under either title, it is a classic.

Walt Whitman

IF THIS NATION WERE ENDOWED with a national religion, its name would be "democracy"; its foremost prophet, Walt Whitman (1819-92); its bible, *Leaves of Grass*; its original sin, slavery; and its redeemer, Abraham Lincoln.

Leaves of Grass is a collection of poems, or better, one long poem with many parts, each one integral to the whole. It was published in 1855, and was revised and enlarged five times, the final or "deathbed edition" appearing in 1892.

In the preface to the first edition, Whitman announced his theme, which would remain constant in all future editions, is this nation. To him, the United States of America is a great poem. And he declared himself its poet.

Whitman's great poem is a perfect complement to *Civil Disobedience*, for whereas the latter asserts and celebrates the diversity of opinion and of free and open discourse upon which the political health of a nation depends, *Leaves of Grass* celebrates something more elemental: the diversity of its people, who are flesh and blood. Whereas Thoreau views our nation as a mighty fortress of ideas, whose weapon is free expression, Whitman perceives a nation incarnate in its people, tangible, many colored, diverse, their manifold sounds and scents filling the air, always rich in expression, relaxed and content in their bodies.

Here, on this continent, "is not merely a nation but a teeming nation of nations. Here is action untied from strings necessarily blind to particulars and details magnificently moving in vast masses" ... a nation whose genius is manifest in the common people, "their manners of speech dress friendships — the freshness and candor of their physiognomy — the picturesque looseness of their carriage ... their deathless attachment to freedom —their aversion to anything indecorous or soft or mean." He celebrates the wonderful leveling of their society and its unlimited diversity; the people have "the air of persons who never knew how it felt to stand in the presence of superiors," which is as it should be for people who are each and all, everywhere and always, free and equal.

It has been remarked by scholars of Whitman's poetry that he used as a model the narrative form of the opening verses of the Book of Genesis. Certainly he echoes the theme of creation, the creation of a nation, of something entirely new that required of him the reinvention of poetry.

> "Stop this day and night with me and you
> shall possess the origin of all poems,
>
> You shall possess the good of the
> earth and the sun .... there are millions of suns left

> You shall no longer take things at
> second or third hand nor look through
> the eyes of the dead nor feed on the
> spectres of books,
>
> You shall not look through my eyes
> either, or take things from me,
>
> You shall listen to all sides and filter
> them from yourself."

And just here is the political connection:

> "One's-Self I sing, a single separate person
> Yet utter the word Democratic,
> the word EnMasse
> Of physiology from top to toe I sing…
> The Female equally with the Male I sing
> Of life immense in passion,
> pulse, and power."

American Democracy as Whitman conceived it is not a system of political authority, or the rule of the majority, which is never perfectly inclusive, and sometimes cruelly exclusive, rather it is a thing organic and whole, and perfectly tangible: a people.

And in this respect, we may consider democracy as a religion for it encompasses the whole of life, in all its concreteness and actuality, its worldly hopes and fears. Whitman put no stock in the great historical religions, and least of all in their supernatural beliefs and expectation of a world to come. likewise, he did not regard body and soul as separate parts of an individual or of a nation, but as vital aspects. The soul is the breath of life, integral to the body. For him, a true democracy is a vital totality encompassing all the people, and thereby it becomes our only comfort in life and death.

Of old age he wrote these lines:

> "I see in you the estuary that enlarges
> and spreads itself grandly as it pours into
> the great sea [of death]."

He also thought that the nation was capable of redemption, and that it had a redeemer: Abraham Lincoln. In 1871, six years after Lincoln's assassination, he summarized his thought in this poem:

> "This dust was once the man,
>
> Gentle, plain, just and resolute, under
> whose cautious hand,

> Against the foulest crime in history
> known in any land or age,
> Was saved the Union of these states."

It is noteworthy also that the only rhymed poem in *Leaves of Grass* is his elegy for Lincoln, *O Captain! My Captain!*

Whether a nation can be redeemed, whether the past can be redeemed, remain open questions, which becomes especially relevant when one takes into account the current state of affairs in this nation, and, beyond it, in the world. One thing is certain: a nation of immigrants that closes its borders to anyone seeking refuge and a better life is in violation of its own principles.

Postscript: The first edition of *Leaves of Grass* is available in a Penguin paperback; the "deathbed edition" is also available in paperback by Vintage. They should by at everyone's bedside. *The Portable Whitman* is also recommended for its ample collection of Whitman's prose writings, especially his *Democratic Vistas*.

VICTOR NUOVO

IMPERIALISM

Manifest Destiny

THE LOUISIANA PURCHASE (1803), concluded by Thomas Jefferson, marks the beginning of the age of American territorial expansion. By 1850 it was nearly complete; the United States of America had become a continental power extending from the Atlantic to the Pacific oceans, "from sea to shining sea." This is a fact that most Americans tend to take for granted. It is enshrined in the well-known anthem "America the Beautiful."

But the means by which this great expansion was accomplished are less well known, which is understandable, for the memory of them is not uplifting or worthy of celebration, even when overlaid with myth. From 1830 to 1850, American westward expansion was accomplished by the forced relocation of native peoples and by a war of aggression against a neighboring country.

Apologists for these actions claimed historical inevitability; they argued that it was this nation's "manifest destiny" to continue westward until it could go no further. An editorial in a New York magazine affiliated with the Democratic Party—the party of Jefferson and Jackson—typified this sentiment by declaring that the time had come for the fulfillment "of our [nation's] manifest destiny to overspread the continent allotted by Providence for the free development of our yearly multiplying millions." It described these millions as an "irresistible army of Anglo-Saxon folk … armed with the plough and the rifle, and marking its trail with schools and colleges, courts and representative halls, mills and meeting-houses." All of this was happening "in the natural flow of events, the spontaneous working of principles." What was foreseen was the formation of a White, Anglo-Saxon, Protestant nation that would soon dominate the continent, and perhaps even the world. It was the seed of American imperialism.

This declaration represents a subtle shift in American political ideology. In the age of revolution and independence from Great Britain, great emphasis was placed on the establishment of a representative democracy subject to the rule of law that would become a model to the world, it was supposed that this development had reached its definitive conclusion in the Constitution by the establishment of a near perfect union in which the people were sovereign.

In the succeeding age it came to be believed that the greatness of a nation resided not only in the nobility of its founding principles, but in the extent of its territory. Land acquisition became paramount, for, it was supposed, noble principles require great space to show themselves! A dubious supposition. Expansion came to be regarded as a right, because it was a "manifest destiny," a divine right, one that is providential, by divine appointment; therefore since God provided for it, it became an imperative, a duty of white

Anglo-Saxon settlers to overspread the land and possess it. In dispossessing its original inhabitants from the land, the settlers believed that they could do no wrong, for they supposed the land was free for the taking notwithstanding its native occupants, and in any case, they had God on their side. The native inhabitants of the land had no right to it, because they were not civilized, they were the mere residue of uncultivated nature, part of the uncultivated landscape, mere pagans.

One wonders, what were the sources of this belief? Did it first arise in the mind of an imbalanced individual who was a nationalist and a racist? Not at all. It is not necessary to go very far back in history to discover its origin. It originated in the early Enlightenment; it is fully articulated by John Locke in his *Second Treatise of Government*, and epitomized in one sentence: "In the beginning, all the world was America."

By "the beginning," Locke means, "a state of nature," a time before unorganized groups of humans had organized themselves into civil societies. According to Locke, civil societies are created only when a body of free and equal persons have agreed by common consent to subject themselves to a common political authority.

Locke assumed that this had not happened in America before the European settlement. America was a political wilderness, in spite of its native inhabitants. In sum, Locke believed that while America was an inhabited land, its original inhabitants were uncivilized, because they had never formed themselves into civil societies, not to mention created learned societies and universities. They existed in a state of nature. Hence, America remained a savage land, and therefore, free for the taking by others, European settlers, who were properly enlightened, or in this narrow dubious sense of the term, "civilized."

Now the social contract theory of the origin of civil society, especially Locke's version of it, is supposed to be one of the gems of the Enlightenment, a standard of political liberalism. But in the minds of America settlers, or their apologists, it was used to justify their right to trump the rights of any others who might dwell in the land.

Would Locke himself have subscribed to these beliefs? Perhaps. It is well known that in 1669 he helped draft the *Fundamental Constitutions of Carolina*. At the time, he was employed by the Earl of Shaftesbury, a leading British politician, as his personal physician and secretary. Shaftesbury was the principal founder of the Carolina colony, which had been granted a royal charter in 1663. The *Constitutions* frame its government and laws. Its system of government is overall feudal and hierarchical; it sanctions slavery and grants to every free citizen the right to possess slaves and to exercise "absolute power and authority" over them. It also mentions "natives of that place," and allows that they "will be concerned in our plantation." It speaks ill of them as pagans, idolaters, ignorant and mistaken, but warns that this is no reason "to expel or use them ill." In sum, Locke seems willing to grant Native Americans protection, but he does not recognize their communities as possessing rights of sovereignty, nor their members worthy to be counted as fellow citizens or freemen.

Postscript: The theme of manifest destiny and western expansion is examined and extolled at length in the celebrated book by the American historian Frederick Jackson Turner, entitled *The Frontier in American History*. The idea of historical necessity is nicely presented and criticized by the British philosopher Isaiah Berlin in *Historical Inevitability*.

The Trail of Tears

THE TERM "TRAIL OF TEARS" TRANSLATES an expression used by the Cherokees to describe their forced exodus from their homeland in northern Georgia and their doleful journey to a place west of the Mississippi River, in what is now the state of Oklahoma. Although there were other native peoples besides the Cherokees who were made to suffer the same ordeal, among them the Chickasaws, Choctaws, Creeks and Seminoles, and others still to come, I focus on their journey because it is well documented, and because the peculiar aspects of this story make it a fitting example of the shameful program of Indian removal pursued by the government of the United States during the 1830s.

Before their removal, the Cherokees were settled in numerous villages in the southern Appalachians, where they had dwelt from time immemorial. It was their homeland.

The English colony of Georgia was more recent, founded in 1730 by royal charter during the reign of George II, from whom it took its name. It sent delegates to the Continental Congress who were among the signatories of the Declaration of Independence. Although slavery was prohibited by its founders, this policy was soon reversed, and the Georgia economy prospered by growing cotton. Its wealth lay in the land, which gave them motive for Indian removal.

A policy of Indian removal was initiated by the government of the state of Georgia in 1829. Its purpose was to provide more living space for the descendants of the American settlers. At the time, the Cherokees who dwelt among them had reorganized themselves into an autonomous nation, which they achieved in a most sophisticated way. I will explain.

During his presidency, George Washington initiated a policy of "civilizing" the native inhabitants of the land. He worried that the spread of American settlers would severely restrict their nomadic mode of life; their very survival required that they become farmers and take up the practice of animal husbandry rather than hunting, which is more land consuming. He hoped that they would abandon their ancient tribal beliefs and customs and convert to Christianity, become acculturated, attuned to divine providence, and therefore better able to accept their fate as a subject people. He hoped that they might come to regard him as their great father and protector, for surely his attitude towards them was paternalistic and, so far, affectionate.

In fact, the Cherokees adapted themselves very successfully to the policy of civilization. But its effect was contrary to what Washington had expected. Rather than lessen, it increased their sense of national identity and provided them with the methods to promote and defend their cause. Most important, they formed themselves into a civil society, adding a page to John Locke. In 1827 they convened a constitutional convention, drafted and ratified a constitution, thereby declaring themselves a sovereign nation. It was a brilliant act of one-upmanship!

Section One, Article One, of the Cherokee constitution is a description of their territory. Section Two declares the sovereignty of the people over the land. Unlike American practice, the territory described belonged to the nation at large. No individual among them could buy and sell land, they owned only what they built upon it or produced from it. Whatever improvements they added were theirs. Some of them grew rich and possessed great estates, and like their White neighbors, they owned slaves.

This sophisticated act of self creation was anxiously observed by politicians and White landholders in Georgia, and it became a cause for alarm, for the land the Cherokees claimed was within the domain of the state of Georgia.

Responding to these events, in 1829–30 the government of the Georgia enacted a pair of laws nullifying the Cherokee constitution and all the laws, rules or customs of the Cherokee nation. The state also asserted its right to the disputed territory and its dominion over every person residing in it. The upshot of the Georgia laws was to make outlaws of anyone belonging to the Cherokee nation and dwelling within the state. The government of Georgia based its actions on Article IV, Section 3 of the U.S. Constitution, which states that "no new states shall be formed or erected within the Jurisdiction of any other State." The Cherokees, they contended, were in violation of the supreme law of the land.

Congress responded by enacting The Indian Removal Act (1830). Andrew Jackson signed it into law, with congratulations to the Congress. It authorized the President to negotiate with "Indians residing in any of the states or territories, and for their removal west of the river Mississippi." On the face of it, it might appear that the Cherokees had a choice in the matter, but they did not. President Jackson presented them with an ultimatum: relocate or assimilate! Cherokee leaders finally agreed to negotiate and relocate, although the decision was not unanimous. A treaty was signed. And soon after, Cherokees were rounded up, corralled and prodded by a military escort, they were removed.

The Trail of Tears describes their exodus; it was not to a promised land. It resulted in the death of 4,000 Cherokees, a quarter of their population. To describe this as an instance of genocide may seem an exaggeration, for the purpose was not extermination but relocation. Nonetheless, it was a most shameful course of events in American history.

Alexis de Tocqueville, who was overall in support of American policy, attributed it to historical inevitability, and wrote a poignant epitaph with which I conclude this essay:

> "The Spaniards were unable to exterminate the Indian race by those unparalleled atrocities which brand them with indelible shame, nor did they even succeed in wholly depriving it of its rights; But the Americans have accomplished this twofold purpose with singular felicity, tranquility, legally, philanthropically, without shedding blood, and without violating a single great principle of morality in the eyes of the world. *It is impossible to destroy men with more respect for the laws of humanity.*"

Tocqueville may not have intended any irony here, but in retrospect, his words evoke a sense of profound irony, what the theologian Reinhold Niebuhr called the irony of American history.

Postscript: Two books by the historian Theda Perdue provide much insight into the subject of this essay: *The Cherokee Removal, a Brief History with Documents,* and *The Cherokee Nation and the Trail of Tears,* co-authored with Michael Green, both are available in paperback editions of modest cost. Consult your local bookstore.

The U.S.-Mexican War

THE COURSE OF THIS NATION'S EXPANSION was brought almost to completion by conquest during the presidency of James K. Polk, a protégé of Andrew Jackson, who favored Jackson's expansionist policies and followed them to the letter. He was known as "young hickory," a chip off the old block. Polk presided over the U.S.-Mexican War (1846–48). Henry Clay, whom Polk defeated in the Presidential election of 1844, judged that Polk incited it, and there is general agreement that he did just that.

The event that provoked it was the annexation of the Republic of Texas in 1845. Mexico won its independence from Spain in 1824, after its own war of revolution. Texas was then a province of the Mexican Republic. It was sparsely populated, and the Mexican government encouraged immigrants from the United States (Anglos who became known as Texians); before long Texians outnumbered Mexicans by a ratio of four to one. They soon came into conflict with the Mexican government led by Antonio Lopez de Santa Anna, an autocrat with imperial ambitions. In 1835–36, Texas declared its independence and engaged in war with Mexico. In the battle of San Jacinto, a Texian army under command of General Sam Houston defeated a Mexican army, led by Santa Anna. The victory was decisive, and Texas won its independence, but it was only virtual, for the government of Mexico did not recognize Texas as a nation.

In 1843, the Republic of Texas sought admission to the United States. President Tyler instructed his Secretary of State to enter into negotiations with Texas, and an agreement was concluded in secret. This soon became public, and statehood for Texas became an issue during the presidential campaign of 1844. Henry Clay, the Whig candidate, opposed it; the Democratic candidate, James Polk, favored it. His justification for admission of Texas was "manifest destiny," which was the central theme of his presidential campaign and of his presidency; after his election he pursued it with zeal and cunning. Texas was admitted to the Union Dec. 29, 1845.

Even after the annexation of Texas, its southwestern border remained in dispute; the Mexican government claimed it was the Neuces River, the United States claimed it was the Rio Grande, which ran south and west of the Neuces.

In February 1846, President Polk ordered General Zachary Taylor to advance with his army south of the Neuces and proceed toward the Rio Grande. Taylor obeyed, and took up a position just north of the Rio Grande, opposite the Mexican city of Matamoras. Mexico responded to this provocation by sending a detachment of cavalry across the Rio Grande where they met and defeated a squadron of American dragoons; those who survived surrendered and became prisoners of war.

News of the American defeat was slow to arrive in Washington. On May 9, even before receiving it, Polk proposed to his cabinet that the United States declare war on Mexico; a message was sent to Congress, and on May 13, 1846, war was declared.

Militarily, the war was a great success. U.S. forces under Zachary Taylor, Winfield Scott, John C. Fremont, Commodore Perry and others were victorious. It was a short, savage war, but the savagery was not only between opposing armies, but also against Mexican civilians. In a report to the Secretary of War, General Scott complained of the savagery of his own troops toward the Mexican people: "Our militia & volunteers, if a tenth of what is said be true, have committed atrocities, horrors in Mexico, sufficient to make Heaven weep & every American … blush for his country. Murder, Robbery, Rape of mothers & daughters, in the presence of tied up males." It was not a good war. It was not a just war. It was an imperial war of conquest. It is no wonder that we have grown forgetful of it.

The consequence of the war was the dismemberment of Mexico. In accordance with the Treaty Guadalupe Hidalgo, concluded in May 1848, Mexico ceded half of its territory to the United States, comprising what is now all or parts of the states of Arizona, California, Colorado, Kansas, New Mexico, Nevada, Texas, Utah and Wyoming. The United States paid Mexico $15 million — at present day values, $450 million, a 30-fold increase, but still a bargain.

One feature of the U.S.-Mexican War that gives it prominence is its pervasive racism; it was epidemic among the American volunteers and of their leaders as well. It infected the minds of statesmen who presided over the war, including those who believed it to be unjust. The celebrated American statesman Henry Clay opposed the war and lost a presidential election because of it. He also lost a son: Henry Clay Jr. was killed in the Battle of Buena Vista.

In November 1847, when the war was near its end, Clay delivered a speech concerning its aftermath. He opposed the advocates of Manifest Destiny who were calling for the annexation of the whole of Mexico. He warned that this would be a grave mistake. "We ought not to forget the warning voice of history, which teaches the difficulty of combining and consolidating together conquering and conquered nations." Mexico would have to be pacified; it would require an army of occupation to accomplish this; there would be constant resistance and continuing bloodshed and no peace.

He cited differences of race and religion as the root of the problem, and compared the conquest of Mexico to the English conquest of Ireland. He noted that the Irish and Mexicans are Celtic and Roman Catholic; the English and Americans are Saxon and Protestant. It would be like mixing oil and water. Besides, the United States has sufficient territory in which to grow. Hence, the United States should leave Mexico to the Mexicans and go west. And so it did, and this racial prejudice went with it; it continues today.

President Polk further facilitated Western expansion by negotiating a treaty with Great Britain in 1846 acquiring the Oregon Territory, thus completing the expansion of the Pacific Northwest. From the point of view of Manifest Destiny, one might expect that he would be regarded as a great President. That did not happen, although as one historian has noted, Polk "worked himself to death" to fulfill this myth. He died shortly after leaving office. Perhaps he felt shame for the suffering he caused. If he did there is no record of it. The shame is ours.

VICTOR NUOVO

CIVIL WAR

The American Civil War

Of all the episodes of American history the Civil War is the most problematic, the most studied, and yet in spite of that, the least understood. It looms large in the American historical landscape, surrounded by a rich mythology designed to conceal its horror and, even more, its shame. It is not merely a thing of the past; it is ongoing; its end is not in sight.

The hot war began on April 12, 1861 and was officially concluded with Lee's surrender to Grant on April 6, 1865. It was a savage war, "fought altogether without moderation", as the late Middlebury historian William Catton aptly put it. Estimates of war dead range from 650 to 850 thousand, counting North and South together. This is more than from all other US wars combined. Many thousands more were wounded and disabled for life, and the shock of battle may never have left those who fought and survived. The South was defeated, its cities and farms devastated, its economy destroyed, and its fate uncertain, its reconstruction necessary.

Why did it happen? Was it inevitable? What was its outcome? What is its meaning?

The American Civil War was occasioned by the secession of seven southern states. South Carolina was the first to secede. At a state convention convened in December 1860, it declared itself a sovereign and independent state, mimicking the Declaration of Independence. Six other states followed suit during the next few months: Mississippi, Florida, Alabama, Georgia, Louisiana, and Texas. They formed themselves into a Confederation, adopted a constitution and a flag with seven stars, and formed a government. They called themselves The Confederate States of America (CSA) and pretended to be a new nation. After the firing on Fort Sumpter, four more states seceded and joined the Confederacy: Virginia, Arkansas, Tennessee, and North Carolina.

Why did these states secede? All were slave-holding states, and they were a minority in the federal union. The majority of states had abolished slavery. The slave states feared that abolition would be forced upon them. Their economy was dependent upon slavery; plantation owners invested heavily in it. Furthermore, slavery, although morally abhorrent even to some slave holders, was essential to their way of life, to their presumed gentility, to their culture. Besides, slavery brought them great wealth. Cotton was a major world commodity, and the South was a major producer of it; it supplied the booming textile industry in Great Britain and New England. To grow and harvest cotton required cheap and abundant labor. African slaves were abundant and cheap. Besides they looked different; they were Black, which was taken by many who were White to mean that they were inferior creatures, not created to be free and equal persons, not fit for citizenship.

The institution of slavery in America was premised on the false belief that not all human beings are free and equal, that some by nature are fit only for servitude, strong in body but weak in mind, that therefore they may be treated as a commodity, as property that can be bought and sold and used at the pleasure of the owner. It was supposed that the Bible sanctioned this monstrous prejudice, as well as Greek and Roman economic theory.

Yet, by the 18th century, it had come to be generally recognized here and abroad that slavery was morally wrong and should be abolished. It became evident that it contradicted the very principles of liberty and equality on which the nation was founded. Even some slave-owners acknowledged this.

To justify continuing the practice of slavery, its defenders invented the false ideology of race and privilege. In his inaugural address as the first and only Vice-President of the CSA, Alexander Stephens declared slavery to be the cornerstone of Confederacy, founded on "the great truth that the negro is not equal to the white man; that slavery--the subordination of an inferior to a superior race--is his natural and moral condition." This was a widely shared prejudice among Whites, North and South; it persists today.

The Confederate states even imagined themselves victims of abolitionists and of their moral sentiments, which is to say, victims of a self-evident moral truth. The South Carolina legislature complained of the "increasing hostility of the non-slaveholding states to the institution of slavery had led them to a disregard their obligations." The obligations referred to pertain to the apprehension and return of escaped slaves. Article IV, section 2 of the Constitution, and the Fugitive Slave Law, enacted in 1850, required states, whether slave or free, to apprehend and return fugitive slaves to their owners. Many free states, among them Vermont, refused to comply.

In the same vein as South Carolina, a Mississippi convention declared "Our position is thoroughly identified with the institution of slavery ... a blow at slavery is a blow at commerce and civilization ... there was no choice left but submission to the mandates of abolition, or a dissolution of the Union, whose principles have been subverted to work our ruin." Alabama accused the government of refusing to recognize the constitutional rights of its citizens to possess slaves. Texas followed suit, expressing the belief that "all white men are and of right ought to be entitled to equal civil and political rights; that the servitude of the African race, as existing in these states, is mutually beneficial to both bond and free". Secessionists accused non-slaveholding states of bad faith in demanding abolition, never bothering to examine the immoral grounds of their own pretended faith.

Lincoln's predecessor, James Buchanan (1791-1868), although a northerner, sympathized with the Southern states, while also condemning slavery in the abstract. In December 1860, in an address to Congress, he blamed the North for the secession of the southern states. "The long-continued and intemperate interference of the Northern people with the question of slavery in the Southern States has at length produced its natural effects." Like many in the North and South, he believed slavery to be morally wrong, yet protected by the Constitution. He also advocated an amendment to the Constitution that would prohibit Congress from passing laws that would abolish slavery or interfere with its practice.

Abraham Lincoln took a conciliatory stance pledging in his inaugural address that he would not try to end slavery in those states where it already existed. He opposed only the expansion of it. He also stated that the Union established by the Constitution was perpetual, which was a warning.

Thus, among the causes of the Civil War were differences over two issues: the institution of slavery and the right of states to secede from the federal union.

Lincoln and Buchanan were conciliatory on the former, but firmly against the latter. They were also obliged to defend the property of the United States and maintain the union. When forces of the CSA demanded the surrender of fort Sumter and proceeded to bombard it, Lincoln called it an insurrection and issued a callup of troops, and the real war began.

Was the Civil War Inevitable?

WAS THE CIVIL WAR INEVITABLE? On the face of it, the answer is obviously No. We label events "inevitable", which we believe cannot be avoided, like death and taxes. But we also believe that human events are the result of choices made by persons who are by nature free, rational, and responsible, who could have done otherwise than they did if they had only chosen to do so, and who might have chosen otherwise if had they had given more careful thought to their options. To suppose that human events are inevitable is to deny that human beings are free agents, capable of deliberate choice, and hence responsible for their actions. It is true that a deed, once done, cannot be undone, that the past cannot be changed. But the irrevocability of the past does not take away from our freedom in the present or our openness to the future, and it does not make us immune from guilt and remorse. What is described as historical inevitability is better cast as the product of human folly and impulsiveness. Secession and war belong in this class.

In any case, regarding the Civil War, in 1861 the Confederate states might have taken Lincoln at his word when he pledged in his first inaugural that he would not interfere with the institution of slavery in any state where it existed;

that the federal government had no right to do so; and that he was not inclined to do it. He offered the Secessionists an olive branch, which they scorned. It could have been otherwise.

Yet these outcomes were unlikely? Perhaps it was an instance of an unstoppable force meeting an irresistible object. In human terms, Secessionist pride, reinforced by fear, came up against Lincoln's determination to preserve the union. Even more, what made the Secessionists afraid was the irresistible moral force of Abolitionism.

Leading Abolitionists were confident that slavery would eventually be ended in the United States, and they fashioned a strategy to achieve it. They were pacifists and believed that war was neither desirable nor necessary; they were sure that there was a better peaceful way to abolish slavery. Emerson, for example, suggested compensating slave-owners for their economic loss if slavery were abolished. They were also moral idealists, confident that justice is an irresistible historical force. Armed with this confidence, and aware of the evident rightness of their goal, they proposed to surround the slave states with a circle of righteousness, which would cause the South to come to its senses and voluntarily to abandon slavery; and, like a scorpion surrounded by a circle of fire, the institution of slavery, being evil, would self-destruct; in the end it would be its own executioner. Abolitionists and radical Republicans adopted this image as a symbol of their purpose and expectation. In their minds, the outcome was certain. Unlike John Brown, most abolitionists did not desire to wield a "terrible swift sword". They feared that a military solution would bring ambiguous results. In retrospect, their fear was warranted.

There is an ironic element in this narrative. the bombardment of Ft. Sumter was a gross strategic blunder by the Confederacy; it sealed its fate and even more surely the fate of American slavery. Lincoln had no other choice but to respond with force. And once the war began it acquired a noble purpose.

James Oakes, a historian at the City University of New York, has developed a theory that the South seceded in order to free itself from the affects of the "circle of fire". They assumed that political separation would make them immune to moral condemnation, that political boundaries would provide them moral sanctuary. They imagined that all that was necessary to prove their immunity was a show of force. They were mistaken; for Justice knows no boundaries, nor does it recognize any force superior to itself.

In his second inaugural address, Lincoln acknowledged the inevitably of the war as a consequence of divine justice. The war was divine retribution, delayed perhaps, but inevitable and devastating. Here is what he said.

"The Almighty has his own purposes. 'Woe unto the world because of offenses! for it must needs be that offences come; but woe to that man by whom the offence cometh!'

"If we shall suppose that American Slavery is one of those offences which, in the providence of God, must needs come; but which, having continued through His appointed time, He now wills to remove, and that He gives to both North and South, this terrible war, as the woe due to those by whom the offence came, shall we discern therein any departure from those divine attributes which the believers in a Living God always ascribe to Him? Fondly do we hope--fervently do we pray--that this mighty scourge of war may speedily pass away. Yet, if God wills that it continue, until all the wealth piled by the bond-man's two hundred and fifty years of unrequited toil shall be sunk, and until every drop of blood drawn with the lash, shall be paid by another drawn with the sword, as was said three thousand years ago, so still it must be said, 'the judgments of the Lord are true and righteous altogether'."

If the war was a demonstration of divine retribution, then the object of divine wrath must have been sin. That sin was slavery, and this nation was immured in it, from its very beginning. Thus, a war of retribution became a national fate.

A Nation "Concieved in Sin"

AMERICAN SLAVERY WAS A CRIME COMMITTED against Black Africans by White Bible-reading Anglo-Saxons, who regarded their victims as movable, disposable property, household animals or livestock, whose only value was in the labor of their bodies. It was a savage institution, unrestrained in its brutality, totally vile. Slave masters and their overseers often took sadistic and prurient delight in beating their slaves, especially if they were women and even more if they were shapely and desirable. American slavery was a crime against humanity, propelled by greed and sustained by a host of other depraved passions; it lasted not just for decades, but for nearly two and a half centuries--the first slaves imported by an English colony were brought to Jamestown in 1619 and the institution of slavery continued through independence until 1865, when it was abolished by the adoption of the thirteenth amendment.

Slavery has been called this nation's original sin. This religious expression is not inappropriate. The biblical roots of the idea lead us to Psalm 51:5, a penitential prayer attributed to King David: "Behold, I was shaped in iniquity, and in sin did my mother conceive me". "Concieved in sin" seems antithetical to "conceived in liberty". And yet both apply to the founding of this nation, and no clear understanding it and of its historical meaning is attainable without pondering this contradiction.

But first, it is necessary to be clear about the meaning of "original sin". The Psalmist's utterance, "in sin did my mother conceive me" must be taken figuratively. It is not about sexuality, but about moral wrongdoing. The Psalmist understood the nature of things. His purpose was to give expression to an evil impulse rooted in an individual's very being, joined by a sense of personal unworth, of shame, remorse, and guilt. The Psalmist's utterance is deeply personal; yet it has universal meaning; it rings true.

Do nations have souls? If by "soul" we mean not a rare ethereal entity that survives death, but a vital spirit that quickens the body and endows it with an inner sensibility, then, I think, they do. To be sure, nations are not persons, but they are convened and constituted by a community of persons who fashion themselves into a civil society, and who do so with serious purpose, and these purposes are conserved and recoverable in the products of civilized life, in a nation's literature, and art, and recorded history. These are the expressions and the artefacts of a nation's soul.

That purpose is expressed in the Declaration of Independence. It was this founding moment that Abraham Lincoln referred at Gettysburg, when he described the birth of this nation, "conceived in liberty, and dedicated to the proposition that all men are created equal." The institution of slavery contradicted this founding, and had done so from the very beginning. Slavery is evil. Hence, it makes sense to join these expressions, when describing the founding of our nation: "conceived in liberty; conceived in sin".

Many who endeavored to found this nation and frame its constitution were slave-holders: chief among them Washington, Jefferson, and Madison. John Adams, Alexander Hamilton, and John Jay were not. Among occupants of the office of president, nine of the fifteen presidents prior to Lincoln were slaveholders. They were also all Christians, committed to the principle of doing to others as you would have others do to you.

William Lloyd Garrison (1805–79), the great abolitionist, regarded slavery as sin, and charged the framers of the Constitution with casting this founding document in favor of slave-owners and their posterity. He charged the framers with making a "covenant with death", an "agreement with hell". He was not exaggerating. By carefully reading the text, scholars have unearthed contradictions in the original text of the Constitution, and in the arguments among the framers. For example, Article I, Section 2, Paragraph 3, provided slave states with greater representation in Congress by counting slaves (or, 3/5 of their number) along with "free Persons" and indentured servants residing in each state. (Unlike slaves, indentured servants serve by contract and for a fixed period of time; they were counted as whole persons.) The 3/5 provision was doubtless a compromise. This provision was repealed by the Fourteenth Amendment.

Article IV, Section 2, Paragraph 3, dubbed the "fugitive slave clause" required that persons in servitude (either indentured servants or slaves), who escape to another state, including free states, must be returned, if the owner demands it. This provision was repealed by the thirteenth amendment. These are but two examples of constitutional provisions that facilitated slavery. There are more, but these are enough to show the impurity of our national beginning.

Garrison proposed to set things right. He demanded immediate abolition as the only proper way to way to eradicate the sin of slavery, and the full integration of free blacks into American society, fully free and fully equal. His position is absolutely consistent; it was and is only right course or path to take, and one that this nation has not yet attained.

The theological narrative of sin runs from wrongdoing to its acknowledgment, repentance, forgiveness, and redemption. To use this sequence as a paradigm of American history, it is necessary for White Americans, even today, to acknowledge the sin of their founders, and its affects, such as racism and numerous other prejudices which are still at work in our misshapen American society, and to pursue the goal of redemption by achieving a society that is inclusive of all, without distinction, where all are free and equal. And what of forgiveness? Its fruition lies in the hope that, in the end, when our society is truly whole, mutual trust and respect of all for all will prevail. One need not be religious to see the point of this narrative of sin and redemption. I believe that it contains the very meaning of our nation's history as it makes its way into the future.

Postscript: In preparing this essay, I have relied on an excellent book by Paul Finkelman entitled *Slavery and the Founders*, and also the notes of James Madison on the first constitutional convention, transcribed with comments in *The Constitutional Convention*, edited by Edward Larson and Michael Winship. Consult your local bookstore. I also recommend the works of David Brion Davis, *The Problem of Slavery in Western Culture, The Problem of Slavery in the Age of Revolution*, and *The Problem of Slavery in the Age of Emancipation*; all in paperback editions, and very readable. Consult your local book shop.

William Lloyd Garrison

THE BEST WAY TO INTRODUCE READERS to William Lloyd Garrison (1805–1879) is to allow him to speak for himself:

> "Assenting to the 'self evident truth
> that all men are created equal', I shall
> strenuously contend for the immediate
> enfranchisement of our slave population …
> I am aware that many object to the severity
> of my language; but is there not cause for
> severity? I will be as harsh as truth, and
> as uncompromising as justice. On this
> subject, I do not wish to think, or speak, or
> write, with moderation. No! No! Tell a man
> whose house is on fire to give a moderate
> alarm; tell him to moderately rescue his
> wife from the hands of the ravisher; tell
> the mother to gradually extricate her babe
> from the fire into which it has fallen;
> -- but urge me not to use moderation in
> a cause like the present. I am in earnest
> -- I will not equivocate -- I will not excuse

-- I will not retreat a single inch -- AND I WILL BE HEARD."

These words introduced the first issue of an abolitionist newspaper, *The Liberator*, which Garrison edited from 1831 until 1865. It became the voice of the Abolitionist Movement in America. They convey a sense of urgency and moral seriousness; indeed, the Abolitionist movement comes as near to moral purity as anything in the history of the world might reach. Its seriousness of purpose and clarity of expression is a perfect antidote to the romance and sentimentality evoked by the popular myth and lore of the American Civil War; it dissipates that misbegotten aura, like a strong wind dispelling the haze and bringing into view the clear sky above, where goodness and justice reign pure and send their radiance into the darkness below. It remains a tonic that we might all try taking in this age of political corruption and moral emptiness.

"Immediate Enfranchisement of our Slave population" was regarded by many as an extreme position, and Garrison was regarded by many as a fanatic. More moderate advocates of abolition favored a gradual approach to this goal and looked askance at complete integration of the Black and White populations; others accepted immediate liberation but advocated a policy of relocation, to another continent. The American Colonization Society was founded in 1821 for this purpose: to relocate free Blacks to Africa, ignoring the fact that most American Blacks were native born Americans. Three American presidents supported the Society: Jefferson, Madison, and Monroe. Garrison at first supported this program but was soon repelled by its shallowness and inherent racism.

What is especially noteworthy about the Abolitionist Movement is the manner in which it promoted its cause. The leading advocates of abolition were constantly on the lecture circuit, but their wider and perhaps most decisive influence was made possible through newsprint. The newspaper as a socially reforming instrument came of age, and Garrison became a master of the medium; it became his body. I am reminded of the late Marshall McLuhan's remark "The medium is the message" But, unlike McLuhan and his heirs--the proponents of social media--Garrison ennobled the medium by making it an instrument of justice.

Garrison was a mere youth of twenty-five when he began his career as an abolitionist. He was impulsive and very quickly became an object of derision among the hoi polloi. In September 1835 a gallows was erected by unknown persons opposite his residence, and a month later a racist mob in Boston attacked him, put a noose around his necks and dragged him through the streets.

One wonders why in Massachusetts, where slavery had been abolished, the villainy of racist mobs should prevail. Why would white males, who had no financial interest in slavery, and a generation later whose sons would go to war to end slavery, behave in this way? And not only the Boston mob, but its aristocracy, with supposedly elevated minds, looked down on Garrison and Garrisonism as crude and unbecoming. Even today, there are historians who treat him as an outside, beyond the mainstream. If that is so, then it may be more a reflection on the deficiencies of the main currents of American thought than on Garrison.

In any case, Garrison's editorials in *The Liberator* contain a catalog of progressive ideas. In addition to his demand for the abolition of slavery, he was an early advocate for women's suffrage. His doctrine of Non-resistance anticipated the teachings and methods of Gandhi and Martin Luther King. He was deficient in one important respect: he ignored the rising labor movement.

He was not perfect. His militancy made him sometimes dogmatic, and he was not always consistent with his own principles, which brought him into conflict with reformers who shared his point of view and supported his causes, among them Frederick Douglass (1818–95), Harriet Beecher Stowe (1811–96), and Wendell Phillips (1811–84). Douglass will be the subject of the next essay; so I will pass by him for the moment and comment here only on the last two.

Garrison was critical of Stowe's depiction of the character of Uncle Tom in her eponymous novel. He found Uncle Tom too forgiving of his masters, and too willing to suffer the miseries of servitude. And yet, as Stowe pointed out in her correspondence with him, Uncle Tom was the embodiment of Garrison's own principle of non-resistance. Garrison's response was that political change required a more militant pacifism. He did not give details.

His quarrel with Wendell Phillips was more substantial. As the war drew to a close, Garrison was more and more drawn towards Lincoln and his conciliatory policies toward the South, and his leniency towards the secessionist states that were now seeking reentry to the Union. Garrison's vision of immediate enfranchisement narrowed; he no longer demanded that, former slaves be granted the full civil rights of citizens, in particular, the right to vote. It was enough that they were free. Phillips would have none of this. He wanted complete integration. There was a parting of the ways. Garrison left the movement; and under Phillips leadership, Abolitionism enlarged into a wider movement for progressive social reform that continues today. More will follow.

Frederick Douglass, The Experience of Slavery

FREDERICK DOUGLASS (1818-95) WAS BORN into slavery, but this pernicious institution could not contain him. Self-educated, except for a brief moment of kindness by a mistress who taught him the alphabet, he escaped slavery and became an influential public orator, journalist, and author, a master of the English language, and a leading public intellectual. If it were not for the color of his skin, he would dominate the intellectual history of 19th century America. Few figures in the history of this nation stand equal to him, there are none who stand above him.

Among his writings are three autobiographies; the first published in 1845, the second, in 1855, and the third in 1893. They provide a thoughtful yet vivid account of what it was like to be a slave.

Frederick Douglass was born in Maryland; his mother was a slave, named Harriet Bailey. He did not know his father or his birth date. Rumor had it that his father was a White man; his master or his overseer. In keeping with the practice of slaveholding, he was removed from his mother's care while still an infant. The practice was designed to prevent the growth of parental affection and attachment, of mother love among slaves. He was nursed by another woman, also a slave. He recalls that his mother was hired out to a neighboring farm ten miles away. She died when he was only seven years old. Of her death he wrote: "I received the tidings of her death with much the same emotions I should have probably felt at the death of a stranger", and adds, "I do not recollect of ever seeing my mother by the light of day." Yet he did recall night visits from her and felt her mother love. "She would lie down with me, and get me to sleep, but long before I waked she was gone". On one occasion, she brought him a cake in the shape of a heart, a Valentine. In a subsequent autobiography, he comments "the pains she took, and the toil she endured to see me, tells me that a true mother's heart was hers, and that slavery had difficulty in paralyzing it with unmotherly indifference." Douglass' comment is a profound condemnation of the institution of American slavery, whose practices were designed to deprive slaves of their humanity and to destroy all human feeling in them except fear. There is nothing redeeming in the practices of American slaveholders; whoever claims otherwise is either deluded or a liar.

When he was eight years old, Douglass' old master died and he became the property of Thomas Auld, who loaned him to his brother Hugh and his wife Sophia Auld to be a playmate for their young son. He was deeply touched by the kindness of his new mistress and by her tenderness towards him, especially when he was in her son's company. She would often read the Bible to them; on one occasion he asked her to teach him to read; she complied and began by teaching him the alphabet and spelling. He learned quickly, and all went well until this were discovered by his new master. He ordered his wife to stop at once and proceeded in the most vulgar terms to lecture her in "the true philosophy of the slave system". In sum, he said that learning spoils a slave. "If he learns to read the Bible it will forever unfit him to be a slave. He should know nothing but the will of his master and learn to obey it." He added, as though to mitigate the harshness of his words, that learning would only make a slave unhappy. Sophia Auld took her husband's words to heart, and their affect on her behavior and her character was tragic. She became more violently opposed to his reading than her husband. If ever she found him reading, she "would rush at me with the utmost fury" and snatch away the book or paper from his hand. All her tenderness towards him vanished. Her kindness was replaced by suspicion; she often spied on him whenever he was alone by himself.

The most revealing parts of Douglass' autobiographies are his analyses of the grim psychological affects of slavery on slaveholders. Their characters became deformed, they ceased to be whole persons.

Douglass returned to the household of Thomas Auld, who then sent him to work on the farm of Thomas Covey, who was reputed to be a "negro breaker"; there he was repeatedly flogged. He fled the "tyrants lash" and went into hiding; but finding no way of escape, he returned. It was a Sunday, and on his return, he met Covey and his wife on their way to Church, "dressed in their Sunday best--looking as smiling as angels". He was greeted benignly. But on Monday, everything was back to normal. While he was in the stable tending to the horses, Covey "sneaked into the stable, in his peculiar snake-like ways" and seized him. He was planning to bind him up and whip him. Douglass resisted. There was a struggle, and he saw fear in the face of his master. Covey called for help, but other slaves, and a hired hand, gave none. After two hours, Covey gave up the struggle and declared a hollow victory. "Now, you scoundrel, go to your work; I would not have whipped you half so much had you not resisted", but in fact, "he had not whipped me at all". And he never tried again. Douglass was 16 years old

The following year, he was "hired out" as a field hand to a Maryland farmer, William Freeland, a more enlightened master, who allowed him more personal freedom, which he used to teach other slaves to read, without his master's knowledge. Douglass later wrote that Freeland was "the best master I ever had, until I became my own master." This soon followed.

When he was 18, he was returned to the Baltimore household of Thomas Auld, who promised him his freedom at age 25 if he learned a trade. He was apprenticed to the master of a local shipyard and learned to caulk wooden ships. But he didn't wait for Auld to keep his promise.

In Baltimore, he met Anna Murray, a free Black woman and with her help he planned his escape to freedom. He made the acquaintance of a retired sailor, a Black Freedman, who loaned him his papers, and on September 3, 1838, Frederick Douglass, approximately 20 years old, became his own master, travelling by train from Baltimore to Wilmington, and by steamer to Philadelphia, and thence to New Bedford, Massachusetts, where he could practice his trade. But he would accomplish much more.

Postscript: Douglass' autobiographies have been collected in a single volume by the Library of America. Also recommended is *The Portable Frederick Douglass*, edited by Henry Louis Gates, Jr. One should also read the *Narrative of Sojourner Truth*, Douglass' contemporary; Truth (1797–1883) was born into slavery in Ulster County, New York, and was freed in 1827 by state law; also there is a recent film about Harriet Tubman (1822–1913), who escaped from slavery and then led many other slaves to freedom; during the Civil War she served as a spy in the Union Army.

A House Divided

In June 1858, the Republican Party of Illinois held its state convention and nominated Abraham Lincoln to be its candidate for the United States Senate. He began his acceptance speech by calling attention to the precarious state of the nation, which was divided over slavery. Like a preacher, he began by issuing a divine warning: "A house divided against itself cannot stand" (Mark 3:25), and continued, "I believe this government cannot endure, permanently half *slave* or half *free*. I do not expect the union to be *dissolved*–I do not expect the house to *fall*–but I *do* expect that it will cease to be divided. It will become *all* one thing or *all* the other."

I imagine that most readers will recall these lines, many may be able to recite them from memory. But I also imagine that most reading this will not recall what Lincoln said before and after. Before, he warned that the agitation against slavery would not cease until "a *crisis* shall have been reached and passed", and that the crisis will only end when the nation "will become all one thing or all the other", that is, *All slave or all free*. His words were prophetic.

He explained the alternatives: "*Either* the opponents of slavery will arrest the further spread of it, and place it where the public mind shall rest in the belief that it is in the course of ultimate extinction; or its advocates will push it forward, till it shall become lawful in all the States, *old* as well as *new--North* as well as *South*."

In retrospect, the crisis has past, and the outcome decided: the union has been preserved and chattel slavery is no more. But in 1858, the outcome may not have seemed inevitable, and the alternatives may have seemed real: one nation, all free, or all slave, the one as likely one as the other.

Lincoln posed this question to any who might doubt this: "Have we no *tendency* to the latter condition?", that is, a tendency towards becoming all slave, a nation in which owning slaves and being enslaved would be permitted in every state. He devotes the remainder of his speech to proving that this possibility is real and as likely to be realized in the future as its contrary, that the United States might well become a slave nation. No doubt, Lincoln had a political motive in arguing this case. The Republican party was new and at its founding it set itself on a mission to end the institution of slavery, sooner or later. The opposite was morally unacceptable to abolitionists.

Lincoln's Democratic opponent was Stephen A. Douglas. He disagreed. He was a strong advocate of westward expansion, as was Lincoln. Douglas was also an advocate of the doctrine of popular sovereignty, whereby the people of every state, old or new, had the right choose whether to permit slavery. He doubted that differences over slavery would divide the states and jeopardize the union.

Lincoln scoffed at the notion of popular sovereignty. He characterized it as "squatter sovereignty", anticipating a distinction that has become commonplace, between Populism and Democratic Republicanism. As he would later put it in the *Gettysburg Address*, "government of the people, by the people, and for the people" is an eternal principle, yet it must be joined to other principles as well, above all, those of liberty and equality for all. Populism outlaws dissent: "if any one man, choose to enslave another, no third man shall be allowed to object." Populism is the tyranny of the majority. Democratic republicanism requires that the people adhere to a rule of law grounded in justice. They are as different as night and day.

Did Lincoln really believe there was a possibility that the nation might become all slave? I don't know. But consider his reasons for believing it. He mentions three events, two, which occurred in 1854, and a third in 1856.

In 1854, Congress passed of the Kansas Nebraska Act. It was sponsored by Stephen Douglas and signed into law by President Franklin Pierce. It established that whether a state or territory should be slave or free shall be decided only by the people of that place, thereby making it possible for slavery to exist in every state or territory, depending on what the majority decide.

In the same year, the Supreme Court issued the Dred Scott Decision. It was written by Chief Justice Roger Taney, and promoted by James Buchanan, who would be elected President in 1856.

Dred Scott (1799–1858) was a slave, whose master had brought him into a free territory. Scott believed that by entering a free territory, he became free. He brought suit against his owner, and his case made its way to the Supreme Court, which ruled 7–2 against him. In effect, the court dismissed the case because Dred Scott, who was a slave of African descent, had in their judgment, no legal standing.

> "We think ... that [black people] are not included, and were not intended to be included, under the word "citizens" in the Constitution…On the contrary, they were at that time [of the nation's founding] considered as a subordinate and inferior class of beings who had been subjugated by the dominant race, and, whether emancipated or not, yet remained subject to their authority, and had no rights or privileges but such as those who held the power and the Government might choose to grant them."

The Court also overruled the Missouri Compromise of 1820, which prohibited slavery in all states and territories north of latitude 36°30.   And finally, it affirmed the principle of popular sovereignty in all territories and states, and therefore prohibited the US Congress from legislating against slavery.

The election in 1858 of James Buchanan, who favored these regressive policies, was the third event. Lincoln even suggested that there had been collusion between "Stephen, Franklin, Roger, and James".

I return to the question—Did Lincoln really accept the possibility that the nation might become all slave? He was aware of powerful reasons for believing it. He feared for the worse. Perhaps, in the light of our current political crisis, we should ask this question of ourselves, have we, as a nation, outgrown the hateful legacies of slavery, racial prejudice and intolerance? It has become a timely question, when populist politics have taken possession of the nation, and prejudices of every variety have become fashionable, infecting the public mind like a plague.

Postscript: Lincoln lost his Senate race to Douglas, whom he would face again two years later in the Presidential contest, which he would win, and through his effort, the house remained standing and slavery abolished.

VICTOR NUOVO

The Politics of Emancipation

IF IT HAD BEEN UP TO HIM, ABRAHAM LINCOLN would not have chosen the title of "The Great Emancipator" for himself. He would have preferred "Preserver of the Union". In 1862, in a letter to Horace Greeley, he made clear that his chief purpose in the war was to "save the Union in the shortest way under the Constitution". "My paramount object in this struggle *is* to save the Union, and *is not* either to save or destroy slavery. If I could save the Union without freeing *any* slave, I would do it; and if I could save it by freeing *all* the slaves, I would do it; and if I could save it by freeing some and leaving others alone I would also do that. What I do about slavery, and the colored race, I do because I believe it helps to save the Union." Having said this, he adds this qualification. "I have here stated you my purpose according to my view of *official* duty; I intend no modification of my oft-expressed *personal* wish that all men everywhere could be free."

Readers of the previous essay in this series may notice that what Lincoln wrote in this letter put him in contradiction with what he said four years before in his House Divided Speech. Then, in 1858, he warned that the nation, in order to survive, must become *either* all slave *or* all free. Now, in 1862, he seems to be saying it could be something of both. The issue of slavery seems to have receded in his consciousness.

What caused the change? In 1858 he was an aspiring politician little known outside his home state of Illinois, addressing an audience a majority of whom were abolitionists, members of a newly formed freedom party. In 1862 he was President of the United States, commander-in-chief of the army and navy, looking for "the shortest way under the Constitution" to overcome an insurrection. In this light the Emancipation Proclamation appears not as a great humanitarian document, but as a weapon of war meant to do economic and material damage to the South. As the historian James Oakes has observed, emancipating the slaves of one's enemy was "an ancient practice" of waging war. The British employed it during the Revolutionary War against rebel slaveholders in Virginia.

This strategic purpose should be clear to anyone who reads the Emancipation Proclamation. It directs that on January 1, 1863, "all persons held as slaves within any State ... the people whereof shall then be in rebellion against the United States, shall be then, thenceforward, and forever free", and it directs naval and military forces to "recognize and maintain the freedom of such persons", and do nothing to prevent them "in any efforts they may make for their actual freedom." Then, addressing those persons emancipated by this decree, he counsels them "to abstain from violence, unless in necessary self-defense" and that "they labor faithfully for reasonable wages". He also allows that these emancipated slaves, if they be "of suitable condition" may enlist in the armed forces of the United States, thereby not only freeing slaves of secessionist owners, but arming them if they would only volunteer to fight for the Union.

Given the dependence of the Southern economy on slave labor, the effect of this action was to deplete the labor force of the Confederacy. Fugitive slaves who managed to cross into Union territory entered it as "freedmen"; the temptation to do so was great, and many did so.

Note that all this applied only to slaves in states that had seceded from the Union. It did not apply to slaves in states that resided in the Union, in the border states of Delaware, Kentucky, Maryland, and Missouri. Their owners were not deprived of their human property.

The Emancipation Proclamation was not Lincoln's final action in this matter. He promoted passage of the thirteenth amendment of the Constitution, which abolished slavery and involuntary servitude in the United States, "except as a punishment for a crime". This was his final act, and he used all the power of the presidency to secure its passage through the Congress, although he would not live to celebrate its ratification. Here we catch a glimpse of Lincoln motivated by principle rather than military necessity, by his "oft-expressed *personal* wish that all men everywhere could be free."

Yet one must not allow sentiment to mislead judgment even here. The Thirteenth Amendment abolished slavery. It did not grant citizenship and the right to vote to former slaves. This was accomplished by the fourteenth and fifteenth amendments, which were introduced after Lincoln's death, and it must remain uncertain whether Lincoln, had he lived, would have given the same vigorous support to their passage.

Sadly, Lincoln was of the opinion that White and Black are better off living separate and apart. For him, the proper sequel to emancipation was colonization of free Blacks to another place, if not Africa, then Central or South America.

On August 14, 1864, Lincoln invited a "Committee of Colored Men" to meet with him at the White House; they were all freemen, leaders of their communities, and although almost all dwelt in Northern states, they did not have the right to vote. His purpose was to recommend that they consider emigration to another place; he suggested Africa, perhaps Liberia, or, if not there, then closer to the land of their birth and life experience, to Central America, in particular, the isthmus of Panama where there were abundant resources for industry and commerce: there was abundant coal on which to build an economy and access to the Atlantic and the Pacific oceans for trade. There they would be welcome and enjoy true equality, which he doubted could ever be realized in the United States.

> "You and we are different races. We have between us a broader difference than exists between any other two races. Whether it is

right or wrong I need not discuss, but this
physical difference is a great disadvantage
to us both, as I think your race suffer very
greatly, many of them by living among us,
while ours suffer from your presence. In a
word, we suffer on each side."

Lincoln supposed that social incompatibility between Blacks and Whites was rooted in nature, that it was an incorrigible condition, which he could not change even if he had a will to do so, which he did not.

He assured the Committee that this was merely a proposal, but he hoped they would consider it, which they, with all due respect, agreed to do.

All of this causes me to wonder just what did Lincoln mean when, in the Gettysburg Address, he spoke of a nation "conceived in liberty and dedicated to the proposition that All Men are Created Equal"?

Gettysburg and Beyond

THE GETTYSBURG ADDRESS OPENS with a reference to the founding of a nation: "Four score and seven years ago, our fathers brought forth upon this continent a new nation, conceived in liberty and dedicated to the proposition that all men are created equal." I concluded the previous essay with this question, what sort of nation did Lincoln envisage when he spoke these words? Did he have in mind one that was racially inclusive, or one that was for Whites only? Here is my answer.

To begin with, one thing is clear, Lincoln understood the proposition "All men are created equal" to encompass all races. Of that, we can be sure. In 1852, in a eulogy for Henry Clay, he denounced advocates of slavery, who claimed that the proposition applied to white men only, that it was a "white men's charter of freedom". He condemned this as a willful misreading.

Of universal human equality, Lincoln was certain; but of the social compatibility of Blacks and Whites, he was not. "There's the rub", which makes understanding Lincoln problematic.

In the same speech, he remarked that Henry Clay, whom he greatly admired, was a founding member of the

American Colonization Society, and he quotes approvingly from Clay's speech on the occasion of the society's founding in praise of returning Blacks to Africa: "There is a moral fitness in the idea of returning to Africa her children, whose ancestors have been torn from her by the ruthless hand of fraud and violence. Transplanted in a foreign land, they will carry back to their native soil the rich fruits of religion, civilization, law and liberty".

It has been noted by scholars that in the opening sentence of the Gettysburg Address, Lincoln misinterpreted, perhaps deliberately, the Declaration of Independence. For the Declaration declares the united colonies to be "free and independent states"; it makes no mention of a nation. Indeed, the colonies united to declare their individual independence from Great Britain, and they united in defense of their freedom; but they did not imagine their union to be a new nation. The Southern states that seceded from the Union defended their action by appealing to this founding precedent, which they believed gave them the right to secede. The Constitution expressed the hope of creating "a more perfect union" of the states. Lincoln maintained that the founding documents, the Declaration and the Constitution, intended a perpetual union of the states, and when he used the term "nation" he meant just that, a perpetual union of states, which it had become his duty to preserve.

To return to the original question: Did Lincoln imagine the new nation founded in 1776 to be a nation of

Whites only? It seems that the nation was founded as such, but did he suppose that it was his duty to preserve it in just this way? This may have been what he preferred, as his remarks to the Committee of Colored Men show. But Lincoln never confused his personal preferences¬—or prejudices—with his official duty. It was his duty to preserve the Union; it was not his duty to transport free Blacks to Africa. Indeed, consistent with his duty, he freed the slaves of Confederate slaveholders and armed them. And as the war wound down, and secessionist states sought to return to the Union, when reviewing their new constitutions, which he insisted must prohibit slavery, he was receptive to the prospect of former slaves receiving the franchise. Lincoln was neither a white nationalist, nor a racist; what he said and did gives no aid to either of these abominations.

Rather, Lincoln was a Unionist, and he labored to create a perfect Union. He knew that it was his duty to do this; it became his destiny.

In an earlier essay (see Page 207), I considered the question whether the Civil War was inevitable. I believe, if that question had been asked of Lincoln, that he would have answered "Yes". Remember what he said in his House Divided Speech, "I believe this government cannot endure, permanently half *slave* or half *free*. I do not expect the union to be *dissolved*—I do not expect the house to *fall*—but I *do* expect that it will cease to be divided. It will become *all* one thing or *all* the other." Remember also that Lincoln believed that slavery was morally wrong, and he shared with Abolitionists a confidence that over time slavery would exterminate itself; like them, he believed that there was a moral force operating in the course of historical events. He hoped that the end of slavery would happen peacefully, but as the divisions over slavery widened, he saw that it would only be ended in war. "And the war came".

In the closing words of his second inaugural address Lincoln spoke of the meaning of the Civil War; he described it as a moment in history, which was governed by divine providence, a war of retribution necessitated by the offence of slavery.

> "The Almighty has his own purposes. 'Woe unto the world because of offences! for it must needs be that offenses come; but woe unto the man by whom the offence cometh!' If we shall suppose that American Slavery is one of those offences which in the providence of God must needs come, but which, having continued through his appointed time, he wills now to remove, and that he gives to both North and South, this terrible war, as the woe due to those by whom the offence came, shall we discern therein any departure from those divine attributes which the believers in a Living God always ascribe to him? Fondly do

we hope--fervently do we pray--that this mighty scourge of war may speedily pass away. Yet, if God wills that it continue, until all the wealth piled by the bondman's two hundred fifty years of unrequited toil shall be sunk and until every drop of blood drawn with the lash, shall be paid by another drawn by the sword, as was said three-thousand years ago, so still it must be said 'The judgments of the Lord, are true and righteous altogether'."

Flawed and fallible though he was, Abraham Lincoln was surely a great man and a founder of the nation. If asked what was the source of his greatness, I would look for it in his understanding of history, its transcendent moral purpose, and inevitability of events, which he did not take as an excuse for inaction, but rather which endowed him with courage to act boldly to preserve the union and to recreate a nation.

Reconstruction

THE TERM "RECONSTRUCTION" WHEN APPLIED TO the aftermath of the Civil War has several uses. The South suffered the loss of its infrastructure: its major cities were laid waste, its railroads torn up; its communication systems destroyed; all these had to be rebuilt. Moreover, its economy was destroyed, not only because of the physical damage caused by invading armies, but also because its primary labor force, which produced its major products for export, was no longer enslaved, but free; they became a free labor force, who, by law, possessed the irrevocable right to negotiate the terms and conditions of their labor. Moreover, although the states that seceded were allowed to retain their political identity, it was required, before they could be readmitted to the Union, that they be reconstituted, and that their new constitutions receive congressional approval and presidential endorsement, and this above all, that they be framed according to the principle of human equality--at least for all men.

Thus, Reconstruction also possessed moral and political uses that applied equally to North and South. In this respect, the entire nation was reconstituted; and, as President Lincoln hoped, there would be a "rebirth of Freedom". The historian, Eric Foner, a leading authority of the subject, describes passage of the 13th, 14th, and 15th amendments as a second founding of the nation. The 13th, ratified in 1865, abolished slavery, the 14th, ratified in 1868, granted citizenship to all persons born or naturalized in the United States, the 15th, ratified in 1870, prohibited any state from denying or restricting the right to vote of any citizen.

But, above all, post Civil War reconstruction required that the very idea of the People of the United States had to be enlarged to include all persons born or naturalized in the United States, regardless of race or ethnicity. Legally, this was accomplished by constitutional amendment. But what remained was the complete implementation of this new law throughout the nation.

To accomplish this, in March 1865, Congress passed legislation creating the Freedman's Bureau; the bill was signed into law by Abraham Lincoln. It became an agency of the US military and functioned very much like agencies created after World War II by the Allied Powers to preside over the reconstruction of Germany and Japan. At its head, Lincoln appointed General Oliver Otis Howard. Howard was acclaimed as a fighting general; he lost his right arm at the Battle of Seven Pines and was awarded the Medal of Honor. He pursued his new duties with energy and moral purpose. His principal goal was to endow former slaves with a sense of their own moral worth and autonomy, and prepare them for economic independence, and to that end he encouraged the creation of Black colleges and churches. He was one of the founders of Howard University, which was intended to train teachers and ministers; he served as its president from 1869-74; the university is named after him. Perhaps the most significant accomplishment of the Bureau was the creation of Black churches, which played a central role in the Civil Rights Movement during the last century. They produced Martin Luther King, and many others heroes of liberty.

But the programs and policies of the Freedman's Bureau did not go unchallenged. The challenges came from two sources, the Neo-Confederate "Redeemers", whose slogan was "The South shall rise again" and whose chief goal was to reduce Freedmen to their former state of servitude, by any means, legal or illegal, often violent; the other came from the office of the President of the United States, Andrew Johnson.

Johnson (1808–75) was serving as US Senator from Tennessee in 1860, when his state seceded from the Union. He chose not to resign his office but remained loyal to the Union. He later served as military governor of Tennessee. Although a Democrat, Lincoln chose him as his running mate on a national union ticket, as part of a strategy to promote postwar reconciliation with the South. It was an unfortunate choice for the nation. When, following Lincoln's murder, Johnson became President, he favored the interests of former slave owners and shared the prejudices of White Supremacists. He demeaned the moral and intellectual capacity of Blacks. Left to themselves, he claimed, they would revert to barbarism. He summed up his position on reconstruction by declaring that

"White men alone must manage the South", as he believed they always did in the North. He vetoed bills to expand the work of the Freedman's Bureau, which Congress overrode.

His struggles with Congress, especially with Thaddeus Stevens, a powerful proponent of the full civil rights of Blacks, led finally to his impeachment by the House. The Senate failed to convict him, falling one vote short of the required two-thirds majority.

The other source of opposition to enlightenment policies of reconstruction came from White Southerners, supported by the indifference of a multitude of White Northerners, many of whom shared the prejudices of their southern compatriots. Their primary political tactic was to introduce legislation in their states to prevent Blacks from voting: poll taxes, residency requirements, complicated procedures to register. Southern legislatures adopted so-called Jim Crow laws, mandating segregated schools, and public facilities. All of these measures were supported by the continuing threat of violence. The Ku Klux Klan, and other similar secret societies, among them, Knights of the White Camelia, and the White Brotherhood, took root throughout the south; they promoted White Supremacy through murder and intimidation. As W.E.B. DuBois observed, "the white laborer joined the white landholder and capitalist and beat the black laborer into subjection through secret organizations and the rise of a new doctrine of race hatred."

In the end, Reconstruction failed to achieve its goals. Eric Foner views it as a source of inspiration. I do not and would revise the subtitle of his history of the period to read "America's aborted second revolution".

Note: the names "Jim Crow" and "Ku Klux Klan" are expressions of the malignant mentality and purpose of the opponents of reconstruction. Jim Crow was a fictional minstrel personality that represented Black men as proverbially stupid and clumsy; Ku Klux Klan is derived from the Greek word *kuklos*, which means "circle"--its purpose to reverse or subvert any just achievement of reconstruction., by violence and intimidation.

Postscript: Eric Foner's *Reconstruction: America's Unfinished Revolution,* and *A Short History of Reconstruction*, are authoritative. W.E.B. DuBois's *Black Reconstruction in America*, is a classic; it sets the proper moral tone to understand Reconstruction. Finally, Henry Louis Gates, Jr., *Stony the Road, Reconstruction, White Supremacy, and the Rise of Jim Crow* is short and powerful. Consult your local bookshop.

Reflections on the Civil War

Normally, I try to write the essays in this series in the third person, as anyone should when writing history. Impartiality is the rule. One's person should not intrude. But I confess that, when reading and thinking about the Civil War, I am constantly overcome by feelings of unease, disappointment, sadness, anger, and shame. With apologies to Julia Ward Howe, whatever glory the Civil War evokes has become tarnished in my imagination.

To be sure, the Confederate insurrection was put down, Confederate armies were defeated, the Confederacy ceased to exist, the Union was preserved, slavery was abolished, the Constitution was amended to grant citizenship to all Freedmen, along with the rights to vote and to equal protection under the law. Yet these noble achievements were not enough to destroy the scourge of racism, which has been and remains today a deadly infection inhabiting the White American mind, creating political fantasies of White nationalism; it knows no borders; its demonic omnipresence pervades north and south. It was the racist fear that slavery might be abolished that caused the South to secede from the Union and make war on the North. Racist beliefs were the means by which slave traders and slave owners eased their consciences of the burden of guilt and the of enormity of their crime, and, finally, it became their consolation in defeat. Racist fantasies were the cause of lynchings and their justification. Racism has been and remains the chief roadblock in the way of achieving full equality by African Americans throughout the nation. It has taken root in our national consciousness, and in this era of acute narcissism and self pity, of passion and irrationality, it has gained new legitimacy in the minds of many.

Considerations such as these lead me to ask whether the Union was worth preserving? And if the answer is Yes, since its preservation required that the Union be victorious in a civil war, whether the Civil War has ended? These are two big questions and require long answers. For the present, I will assume that the answer to the first question is affirmative; postponing until later a justification for it. With respect to the second question, my answer is No, because racism persists.

The historian James McPherson concluded his award-winning narrative of the Civil War *(The Battle Cry of Freedom)* by asserting that the Union victory "destroyed the southern vision of America and ensured that the northern vision would become the American vision". In general this may be true, but it is nevertheless misleading.

In the first place, just what was "the northern vision"? Was it a pure vision of equality? Such a vision surely existed somewhere in the North and even in the South, but it was not the vision of the whole North, neither then nor now, but only of a few enlightened individuals. I am reminded of

Lincoln's belief that it would be better if Black and White did not live together, and of his counsel to free Blacks that they consider emigration to Africa; and of Julia Ward Howe, who wrote The Battle Hymn of the Republic to commemorate the legacy of John Brown, but, in spite of her strong advocacy for the emancipation of slaves, she wrote in one of her books that Blacks are not equal to Whites intellectually or morally; for this she was rightly rebuked by the Abolitionist William Lloyd Garrison; but he in turn later sacrificed his moral vision to political compromise.

Nor did a northern vision make the North immune to racial prejudice and violence. Where was it in 1863 when the draft riots erupted in New York City? Why had it not penetrated the minds of White working-class men, mostly of Irish descent, and prevent them from rioting, tearing up paving stones and hurling them through glass windows, setting buildings aflame, and attacking fire fighters who rushed in to extinguish them, and from murdering 100 innocent Blacks, and destroying their homes and businesses. This nation of immigrants, who were themselves objects of discrimination, had become a racist nation.

There is also a softer subtler, more insidious "southern vision" that lives on and which has infatuated the American mind, north and south. In 1940, when Hitler's armies had overrun Europe, David O. Selznick, a northerner, produced *Gone with the Wind,* based on a novel by Margaret Mitchell, a southerner of Scottish descent. It gave new life to the romance of the Confederacy, depicting slavery as a benevolent institution, and slaves as willing participants in it, devoted to their masters. Selznick worried over the racist theme of the movie, but chose to produce it anyway. In 1942, MGM released *Tennessee Johnson*, which portrayed Andrew Johnson as an American hero. In 1946 Walt Disney, also a northerner, produced *Song of the South*, a racist film. These films were supposed to uplift the nation in time of war, which it fought with segregated armed forces.

The romance of the Old South, which such films depict, is linked to the myth of the Lost Cause. It is claimed that the Cause for which the South fought was a noble social ideal, gentle, cultivated, and chivalrous. Never mind that it was founded on slave labor. Southern romantics supposed that the South lost the war not because its cause was unjust, but because it was overwhelmed by the material superiority of the North. They regarded the war as a conflict of matter against spirit. In the wake of such delusions, much popular Civil War history has been written. Robert E. Lee is touted as superior to Grant as a military leader. It is supposed that Grant was victorious only because he had the benefit of more men and material, which he recklessly expended. All this in spite of the fact that Lee was outgeneraled by Grant in Northern Virginia and by Meade at Gettysburg. How does one explain that Lee has become an icon, while Grant has not? Is it because of Lee's aristocratic manner and appearance compared to Grant's plebeian dishevelment? Yet by making war against the United States, Lee committed treason.

The myth of the Lost Cause is supposed to convey the moral superiority of the Old South over the North. It is the sacred doctrine of Neo-Confederates, where it continues to be put to political use. It was employed by Dixiecrats against Harry Truman. The late Strom Thurmond promoted it. It continues to inspire White Nationalists. In 1993, a bill was introduced in the US Senate by Jesse Helms to grant the United Daughters of the Confederacy patent rights to their corporate insignia, a Confederate Battle Flag encircled by a wreath. After a speech by Carol Mosely Braun, in which she reminded the Senate that the real question at issue was race, the measure was defeated. Senator Mosely Braun reported that, after the vote, as she and Helms rode the elevator together, Helms smiled at her and began singing Dixie.

Has the Civil War ended? I think not. Nor will it end until every trace of racism has been removed from the consciousness of Americans, and White nationalism has become a distant memory, and the Old South regarded as a world well lost.

VICTOR NUOVO

EXPANSION AND SOCIAL REFORM

Reflections on the Frontier

IN 1893, IN COMMEMORATION OF THE 400TH anniversary of Columbus' discovery of America, the City of Chicago hosted a World's Fair, appropriately named The Columbian Exposition. It was a celebration of the world's achievements in science and industry, architecture, literature, and the fine arts and to the progress of American civilization. Among the events marking the opening of the Fair were academic lectures, among them a scholarly paper read by a young historian from Wisconsin, Frederick Jackson Turner (1861–1932), entitled "The Significance of the Frontier in American History". The title summarized his thesis, which has since become known among historians as "the frontier thesis". Turner began by observing that geographically, there was no longer any physical frontier, which is to say, a boundary beyond which there was land free for the taking. Nevertheless, he asserted that the frontier was alive and well, for the very idea of it had taken root in the mind of the nation and become determinative of American national identity. What memory is to personal identity, history is to a nation. The popular history of the frontier had become the ruling narrative of the nation, for good or for ill, the ruling symbol of American purpose and values, and the hallmark of the American character.

Turner's paper became a defining moment in American historiography. Even now, after much critical discussion, it is well worth pondering.

Turner conceived of the American frontier not as a settled boundary but as a moving line, which, from the founding of the nation until the close of the nineteenth century, headed West. The first frontier was the Atlantic coast, then the Alleghenies, next, the Mississippi River, thence it made its way across the Great Plains, to the Rockies, passed through the Great Basin and reached its limit at the shores of the Pacific. Reading Turner is a good primer in geography.

But to be the source of all that he claimed for it, Turner imagined the frontier to be something more than a geographical line. He imagined it as the symbol of a form of life, whose vitality flowed from the promise of free land beyond the frontier, which continued to move west–imagine wagon trains moving across the prairie, or the railroad. And even after the frontier had reached its limit and became a fixed boundary, Turner supposed that it continued to shape the American character, for good or for ill.

What gave shape to this form of life were the circumstances of its beginning. Every westward movement involved a departure from civilization and a return to primitive conditions; the pioneer exchanged his European dress for the hunting shirt and moccasin; he travelled in a birch bark canoe; he lived in a log cabin; and planted Indian corn. There was a recurring need to reinvent civilization, which may not have always involved reinventing the wheel, but surely refashioning it and refitting it, transforming it into an instrument of power. Yet this recurrent return to primitive conditions left a residue of harshness or coarseness in the moral and political character of America that remains today. It is evident in the extremes of populism of the left and right.

Hence the proviso, for good or ill, is a necessary refrain. "So long as free land exists", economic opportunity exists for those willing to seize it, and with it comes political power, and from this a form of democratic polity that borders on populism. Which led Turner to issue this warning: "the democracy born of free land, strong in selfishness and individualism, intolerant of administrative experience and education, and pressing individual liberty beyond its proper boundary, has its dangers as well as its benefits." He worried that Individualism in America had encouraged a corrosive suspicion and hostility towards government, raised private right above civic responsibility, encouraged demagoguery, elevated the spoils system over the rule of law, and other political wrongs.

The poet, Carl Sandburg captured the ambivalence of the culture of the frontier in his poem "Chicago"

> "Hog Butcher for the World,
> Tool Maker, Stacker of Wheat
> Player with Railroads and the Nation's
> Freight Handler;

Stormy, husky, brawling,
City of the Big Shoulders:

They tell me you are wicked and I believe them, for I have seen your painted women under the gas lamps luring the farm boys.

And they tell me you are crooked and I answer: Yes, it is true I have seen the gunman kill and go free to kill again.

And they tell me you are brutal and my reply is: On the faces of women and children I have seen the marks of wanton hunger.

And having answered so I turn once more to those who sneer at this my city, and I give them back the sneer and say to them:

Come and show me another city with lifted head singing so proud to be alive and coarse and strong and cunning.

Flinging magnetic curses amid the toil of piling job on job, here is a tall bold slugger set vivid against the little soft cities;

Fierce as a dog with tongue lapping for action, cunning as a savage pitted against the wilderness"

Turner's warning and Sandburg's brash celebration of Chicago could have been written yesterday. "The more things change, the more they remain the same."

Finally, the history of the moving frontier is one of conquest and of violence, for the land beyond the frontier was never free for the taking. Among the sources I have used in preparing this essay is a trilogy by the historian Richard Slotkin that narrates the history of the Frontier from the seventeenth through the twentieth centuries; the titles almost tell it all: "Regeneration through Violence", "The Fatal Environment", "Gunfighter Nation". Slotkin's long and detailed, yet very readable volumes, offer proof of Turner's thesis. He shows the presence of the frontier myth in our national culture from James Fenimore Cooper's Leatherstocking tales through accounts of Custer's last stand, and on into the 20th century.

Postscript: Turner's original paper, along with others on the same theme in a volume entitled *The Frontier in American History.* It is available in paperback. Visit your local bookshop.

How the West Was Won

BASIC TO THE IDEA OF THE FRONTIER is the belief that beyond it, wherever the frontier happened to be in the course of our nation's westward expansion, there is always more land to be settled—a promised land, which is free for the taking; in the minds of some adventurers, it was the place of El Dorado, the legendary city of gold. This promised place became the central theme of narrative of western expansion. In its retelling, the frontier was transformed into a place of a national epic, whose dimensions were huge and vast and untamed, like the nation itself. It became the focus of the great American myth, "the myth of the frontier". And then Hollywood discovered it, and made it the theme of many films, culminating, in 1962, in Metro-Goldwyn-Mayer's epic film, "How the West was Won" featuring an "all star cast", narrated by the late Spencer Tracy, who concludes with this coda, which represents it as a transfiguration:

> The west that was won by its pioneers,
> settlers, adventurers is long gone now. Yet
> it is theirs forever, for they left tracks in
> history that will never be eroded by wind
> or rain– never plowed under by tractors,
> never buried in compost of events. Out

>of the hard simplicity of their lives, out of
>their vitality, of their hopes and sorrows
>grew legends of courage and pride to
>inspire their children and their children's
>children. From soil enriched by their
>blood, out of their fever to explore and be,
>came lakes where once there were burning
>deserts–came the goods of the earth; mine
>and wheat fields, orchards and great lumber
>mills. All the sinews of a growing country.
>Out of their rude settlements, their trading
>posts came cities to rank among the great
>ones of the world. All the heritage of a
>people free to dream, free to act, free to
>mold their own destiny.

This was the myth of Manifest Destiny refashioned for the big screen, the frontier thesis incarnate, "made flesh". Frederick Jackson Turner might have felt vindicated.

But the land beyond the frontier was neither free nor unsettled. Nor was it a savage place. An Indian wearing moccasins was not a savage, though a White Man may have been. If there was any savagery, and there was an abundance of it, it arose from this nation's Western expansion, which was a phase of the European expansion that began with Columbus, who was inspired by the Renaissance–"the age of discovery". Thus, savagery was a product of European colonization and its westward expansion, the effect of European civilization as it went about colonizing the world. Ultimately, the European Renaissance was the source of the meaning of "the myth of the frontier".

The place of this myth is the Great Plains, that vast territory extending from the Mississippi to the Rockies, The Prairie, which was first peopled by emigrants, who crossed over from Asia over 10,000 years ago and became the first settlers of North America. They were well settled when the first European settlers appeared. They were not savages, rather over millennia they had become properly "indigenous", which is to say, they regarded themselves as natural products of the land.

The 19th century was the great age of territorial and industrial expansion in the United States. Richard Slotkin, the foremost historian of the myth of the frontier, has aptly entitled his history of it, *The Fatal Environment*. His purpose is not to celebrate the myth, but to demythologize it, to reduce it to history, which is the way that all myths should be regarded if truth be told. To represent it, he chose one of its most celebrated heroes, George Armstrong Custer, and its incarnation, Custer's last stand at the battle of Little Big Horn, which Hollywood refashioned in the patriotic film "They died with their boots on", released in 1941, starring Errol Flynn in the title role.

But all of this is mere window dressing concealing the troubling narrative at the heart of the myth that comes to light when it is reduced to history; it is all about the treatment of indigenous peoples. It is a tragic tale, in many cases reprehensible, even when it is well meant.

In this respect, a more suitable symbol for the myth of the frontier is Col. Richard H. Pratt (1840–1923). Like Custer, he served with distinction during the Civil War, and afterward took part in the so-called Indian Wars on the Great Plains. He played a leading role in implementing the federal policy of assimilation of indigenous peoples initiated during the last decades of the 19th century. Among the institutions employed were government boarding schools, whose purpose was to Americanize native American children. Pratt founded and headed one of these and became a leading spokesman for its aims and purposes. In a speech delivered in 1892 he summarized their purpose:

> "A great general [Philip Sheridan] has said that the only good Indian is a dead one, and that high sanction of has been an enormous factor in promoting Indian massacres. In a sense, I agree with the sentiment, but only in this: that all the Indian there is in the race should be dead. Kill the Indian in him, and save the man."

Which leads one to wonder what Pratt believed "man" to be?

Pratt may also have been the first to use term "racism" in common discourse. To his credit, he named it to condemn it, which illustrates the profound moral ambiguity and irony of the history of this nation's western expansion and in our discourse about it.

Slowly, the myth of the frontier receded in American consciousness, until July 1960, when John F. Kennedy accepted the Democratic presidential nomination and declared the opening of a New Frontier; he imagined a frontier not bordering on land, but on new economic and political opportunities, scientific discoveries, and technological improvements. Subsequently, at Kennedy's inauguration, Robert Frost added to this the frontier myth in a poem that he recited at Kennedy's inaugural ceremony, sounding the theme that "The land was ours before we were the land's"; he advocated surrender to the land as the fulfillment of our destiny:

> "Something we were withholding
> made us weak
>
> Until we found out that it was ourselves
>
> We were withholding from our
> land of living,
>
> And forthwith found salvation
> in surrender.
>
> Such as we were we gave our-
> selves outright
>
> (The deed of gift was many deeds of war)

> To the land vaguely realizing westward,
> But still unstoried, artless, unenhanced,
> Such as she was, such as she will become,

These are indeed high-sounding words, but their effect is to conceal the moral ambiguity that lies beneath the myth of the frontier.

American Imperialism

THE UNITED STATES FOUGHT TWO WARS of conquest during the 19th century. The first (1846-48), against Mexico added new territories to the Southwest, which would later be incorporated into the United States. A half century later (1898), it fought the second against war Spain and acquired more new territories: Guam, The Philippines, and Puerto Rico; it also became guardian of Cuba, which later became an independent nation, whose government the US would unsuccessfully attempt to remove by force in 1961. The Philippines won international recognition as an independent nation in 1946, after a half-century of often brutal colonial rule by the US, and for a brief interval, by Japan. Guam and Puerto Rico remain U.S. territories.

Two other territories were acquired beyond the continental boundaries of the forty-eight states. In 1894 the U.S. minister to the Kingdom of Hawaii conspired with American settlers there to overthrow the monarchy. They successfully carried off a coup d'etat, deposed the monarch, Queen Lili'uokalani, and declared Hawaii an independent republic; in 1898, President William McKinley signed legislation annexing Hawaii as a US territory. It became the 50th state in August 1959, following Alaska, which was admitted as the 49th state eight months before. Alaska, which had been a US Territory since 1867, was not acquired by conquest but by purchase, from imperial Russia.

Two wars of conquest, a host of wars against the western Indian nations, a purchase from an imperial power, a coup, colonial rule, a civil war: in the light of all this, I am inclined to describe the second half of the 19th century as a period of imperial expansion.

Strictly speaking, the United States is not an empire. The standard definition of an empire is a vast territory acquired by conquest and ruled by an absolute monarch. Only the first part of the definition fits--although the fantasies of our former chief of state suggest a trend toward completeness.

Nevertheless, during the era from the Civil War to 1900, the Gilded Age, this nation underwent a surge of industrial and economic growth, carried out by entrepreneurs who operated without regulation to achieve their economic goals, monopolizing commodities, trade, and production. This was the era of robber barons, so-called captains of industry: Cornelius Vanderbilt, John D. Rockefeller, Andrew Carnegie, to name a few. They exercised bare economic power ruthlessly and absolutely. They achieved their goals by degrading the natural environment and exploiting labor. It was a display of raw economic power; and they grew enormously rich by it. And there is no doubt, this nation became a great power because of their actions, an empire without an absolute monarch, but led by businessmen whose wealth and financial genius made them absolute rulers of their domains. And by this means, this nation exercised dominion throughout the world. Unlike Rome, it did not require armies to extend its rule. It conquered by ruthless entrepreneurship.

It is also worth remembering that this era of American imperialism coincided with the latter part of the Victorian Age, during which Britain encompassed the world. It was an era of triumph for English speaking peoples.

Yet, during the same era, the nation underwent a great increase of population through emigration of peoples who were not English speaking; immigrants from Southern and Eastern Europe. To memorialize this, a Statue of Liberty was erected in New York Harbor, a gift "from the people of France to the people of the United States". It bears this inscription taken from a poem by Emma Lazarus, written in 1883, entitled "The New Colossus", which I quote in full:

Not like the brazen giant of Greek fame,

With conquering limbs astride from land to land;

Here at our sea-washed, sunset gates shall stand

A mighty woman with a torch, whose flame

Is the imprisoned lightning, and her name

Mother of Exiles. From her beacon-hand

Glows world-wide welcome; her mild eyes command

The air-bridged harbor that twin cities frame.

"Keep, ancient lands, your storied pomp!" cries she

With silent lips. "*Give me your tired, your poor,*

Your huddled masses yearning to breathe free,

The wretched refuse of your teeming shore.

Send these, the homeless, tempest-tost to me,

I lift my lamp beside the golden door!"

Only the last four lines, here printed in italics, appear in the inscription. Lazarus wrote the poem as part of a fund-raising effort to pay for the pedestal of the statue.

A colossus is a sculpted figure larger than life, which is supposed to represent the imagined political power of a nation. The "Greek colossus" to which Lazarus referred, otherwise known as the Colossus of Rhodes, was created as a monument to military might. Lazarus imagined the American colossus to represent something very different. Her colossus is a woman, a "Mother of Exiles", who welcomes the persecuted masses, Europe's "wretched refuse". At the same time, she looks with scorn towards the imperial pomp of old Europe.

"Empire of Liberty" is the title of a book written by the American historian Gordon Wood. The volume deals only with the founding of the nation, but its title might even better describe what the United States, guided by its better angels, was striving to become during this period: a welcoming place, where people throughout the world, seeking safety might find refuge, a nation of immigrants, no longer purely white, Anglo-Saxon, and Protestant, but polyglot and multicultural. This was Emma Lazarus vision of America. And if the vision had become a reality, the empire of United States would be a very different empire from any that the world has ever seen. And perhaps it is to some extent, to the extent as it has opened its borders to peoples needing a place where they may be safe, a sanctuary, and the opportunity to live a good life.

But Emma Lazarus was a victim of anti-Semitism. Indeed, during the late 19th and early 20th centuries, reaction to the flood of emigrants found expression in ever new vile prejudices: against Catholics, Eastern and Southern Europeans, Orientals and more. These hateful prejudices coalesced with the American original sin of racism. And, if one were to fast-forward to the present, we should add Islamophobia, and prejudice against Hispanics. "Empire of Liberty" is a fitting expression, only if it said ironically.

Remembering the Ladies

EARLY IN THE SPRING OF 1776, as the Continental Congress met in Philadelphia to consider what steps to take towards independence, Abigail Adams wrote to her husband John to express her zeal for independence: "I long to hear that you have declared an independency"; and to make a suggestion: "And, by the way, in the new code of laws which I suppose it will be necessary for you to make, I desire you would remember the ladies"; and she added a warning: "Remember all men would be tyrants if they could ... If particular care is not paid to the Ladies we are determined to foment a Rebellion, and will not hold ourselves bound by any Laws in which we have no voice or Representation."

John responded to Abigail's letter by making light of it. He suggested that male dominance was more theory than reality, that in reality women are the true masters. "We [men] are [your] subjects. We have only the Name of Masters" and "to give up this...would completely subject Us to the Despotism of the Petticoat."

He also worried that an incautious move towards independence would "loosen the bands of government everywhere." This was a common fear among the founders, all of them men.

In the end, history would prove Abigail right. But it would take almost three-quarters of a century before the rebellion came. It came in the form of women's rights convention, which met in Seneca Falls, New York, on July 19–20, 1848. The moral fervor of Abolitionist Movement was a source of its inspiration.

Its chief result was a document, *A Declaration of Sentiments and Resolutions*, written by Elizabeth Cady Stanton (1815–1902), a principal organizer of the convention. Stanton was a well-educated patrician; a graduate of Emma Willard's school, she read law with her father who was a prominent jurist, but she was not allowed to take the bar examination. Lucretia Mott (1793–1880) was another organizer; she was an abolitionist and Quaker activist. Frederick Douglass attended the convention and delivered one of the principal addresses.

Stanton fashioned the Seneca Falls *Declaration* after the *Declaration of Independence* and borrowed heavily from it. It was a declaration of women's social, political, and economic independence. She began by declaring that "the inalienable rights of life liberty and the pursuit of happiness" are the rights not only of all men and but of all women, and that whenever any government is destructive of these ends, "it is the right of those who suffer from it to refuse allegiance to it", the right to rebel.

She then proceeded to itemize the reasons for rebellion and began with this observation: "The history of mankind is a history of injuries and usurpations on the part of man toward woman" whose sole purpose was to establish "an absolute tyranny over her." She followed this with a list of every woman's grievances. Men who are the sole lawgivers of this nation have denied a woman's right to vote, so that she has no representation in government. Nor is it different in the family. In the eye of the law, marriage makes a woman civilly dead [Note: When she married, Stanton refused to take the infamous vow of obedience]. In effect, American civil law is unjustly patriarchal. She notes that divorce laws favor the interests of husbands and limit a woman's right to property; that men have monopolized all profitable employments in life; the learned profession is men's exclusive domain as are the best schools. Finally, she noted the deep psychological harm that men have inflicted on women: they have "endeavored… to destroy [woman's] confidence in her own powers, to lessen her self-respect, and to make her willing to lead a dependent and abject life."

Everything that she wrote is true, and if her words caused fear and anxiety in the hearts of any men, then or now, it is discomfort well deserved.

It should be no surprise to any who read her writings that Elizabeth Cady Stanton became the chief philosopher of women's rights movement. The power of her mind and the depth of her insight into human nature and history is evident in them, and irresistible. She rightfully deserves the title of great American philosopher (see the next essay). The writings of Elizabeth Cady Stanton inspired Susan B. Anthony (1820–1906), and what followed was a powerful coalition of thought and practice that shaped the woman's suffrage movement in the 19th century.

But the primary goal, a woman's right to vote, was not attained in that century–the 19th amendment that established this right was not ratified until 1920. The crisis of the Civil War intervened. After the war, as Congress deliberated the 14th and 15th amendments of the Constitution Stanton became embroiled in conflict with abolitionists. It should be remembered that the 14th amendment granted citizenship to all Freedmen; the 15th amendment granted them the right to vote. Stanton believed that the time had come to grant the right to vote to women as well as men. This did not happen, in spite of her eloquent demand.

Her failure to carry the day caused her deep anger. It was indeed a righteous anger, for she rightly saw that the goals of the Seneca Falls *Declaration* were to be achieved only if women were fully enfranchised to vote and hold government office, only if women, like men, had access to the power of government as fully enfranchised participants would they gain the standing of autonomous, sovereign persons, which was their right. If this were denied, then little would be gained.

But her anger clouded her judgment, and she railed against those who had just emerged from slavery, who were victims themselves with just grievances. She failed to recognize the sisterhood she might cultivate with Black women. And she allowed her anger to find expression in what she wrote and said. In short, she used racial epithets and succumbed to this nation's original sin. It was against her better judgment.

Postscript: Two excellent volumes provide selections Stanton's writings with commentary: *Elizabeth Cady Stanton, Feminist as Thinker*, edited by Ellen Carol DuBois and Richard Candida Smith, and *The Elizabeth Cady Stanton–Susan B. Anthony Reader.* Consult your local bookstore.

The Mind of Elizabeth Cady Stanton

ELIZABETH CADY STANTON WAS NOT ONLY a pioneering feminist activist, but she was also a philosopher of great sophistication and deserves to be remembered as such. This is amply demonstrated in her writings, two especially, which I shall review here: *The Woman's Bible* and *The Solitude of Self*. She published them close to the end of her life. The former is a collection of critical essays about the Bible written by Stanton and other women scholars enlisted by her. The other is an address first delivered to the US House Judiciary Committee in 1892, and subsequently to the annual convention of the National American Woman's Suffrage Movement.

Stanton turned her attention to the Bible because it was commonly supposed that it contained proof that women are inferior to men and therefore should be ruled by them. Those who clung to this belief were mostly men with standing in the community, Protestant clergymen, who officiously cited Genesis 2:5-3:24 as sufficient proof. There it is written that after God created Man from dust of the ground (*adam* from *adamah*), he created a Woman from the Man's rib; she was meant to be his helper, and the Man named her Eve, as a token of his dominion over her. In he same story, Eve is blamed for having brought evil into the world by disobeying

God's command not to eat any of the fruit of the Tree of the knowledge of Good and Evil and by persuading Adam to do the same. This was supposed to be proof enough to uphold the prejudice of woman's inferiority.

Stanton noted that the Book of Genesis contains another story about the creation of mankind that comes before the one previously considered. In the first chapter of Genesis, it is written that God created Man in his image, "male and female created he them", which is to say that the term "Man" signifies here not just a male human animal, but a species of dual sexuality, "male and female"; moreover it implies that the "image of God" is likewise "male and female; In sum, God is essentially bisexual. Stanton also noted that the names of God differ in the two chapters. In the first, God is called *Elohim*, which is a plural noun, properly translated "Gods" or the council of the Gods. In the second, God's name is *Jahweh Elohim* (Jahweh of the Gods). This duality of names is common throughout the Bible, and a comparison of the several narratives reveals a difference in theology. Whereas *Jahweh* as a national God is anthropomorphic and patriarchal, beset by the foibles of patriarchy, *Elohim,* The Gods, or the Godhead, represents the council of Gods, as it were, the highest seat of wisdom in the universe, and therefore, properly the creator of heaven and earth. "Thus", Stanton concludes, "Scripture [in its wiser and more coherent places], as well as science and philosophy, declares the eternity and equality of sex". The inconsistency in the Bible requires that it be made subject to the higher authority of reason and common sense, from which it is evident that "The masculine and feminine elements, exactly equal and balancing each other, are as essential to the maintenance of the equilibrium of the universe as positive and negative electricity".

The Solitude of Self goes more deeply into the theme of human equality and discovers its roots in human individuality, which, Stanton's observes, each one of us can discover in ourselves.

How is this so? Because every woman is a human being, and since every human being is a unique individual, each woman must decide her fate, and therefore the entire world must be made open to her, for human self consciousness has no horizons. The same can be said also of every man as of every woman. And that is just her point.

The chief property of being human is self-consciousness, a state of being whereby every individual is altogether alone, where everyone is absolutely oneself. She regards this condition as sublime, awesome, terrifying, and yet also wonderfully fascinating. In her address, she appeals to all human beings to discover this awesome, indeed Godlike quality in themselves.

Stanton was not the first philosopher to write about the idea of human selfhood. The modern philosopher is commonly credited with giving it prominence was John Locke (1632–1704). In 1690, he published An *Essay Concerning Human Understanding*, which has become a philosophical classic. In it, he endeavored to explain how we come to acquire all the knowledge we possess, and his answer was "through experience", by the perceptions of the senses, but also by the capacity we have to examine ourselves; and having discovered the world around us and the self within, to find oneself in a position to reflect upon what it all means?

Moreover, it is through their own self-consciousness that individuals discover their unique identity as persons. When I awake each morning, I remember that I am myself, the same person, even if I may not immediately recall where I am. And even in my dreams, I am conscious of myself acting or observing, for even when dreaming I am directly aware of myself; which is why, waking out of a nightmare brings such welcome relief.

Individual self-consciousness is also the basis of morality. We have the unique capacity to examine ourselves, judge ourselves, determine what is right, feel remorse whenever we fail to do it, and having acknowledged our moral successes and failures, to continue resolute to persevere in the right.

All of this was well known to Elizabeth Cady Stanton, for she was an omnivorous reader, and she most likely read Locke carefully and appropriated much of what he wrote about the self. For example, Locke described the self metaphorically as a solitary voyager sailing his craft on the ocean of being. Stanton seized upon it and filled it with new meaning. Hence the title, *The Solitude of Self*. The self, like a voyager alone on an endless ocean must decide its own fate, for there is no one else to decide it. And this remains so, even if there are any many other selves, and they should join together in families or civil societies. They are obliged to treat each other as free and equal, for self-sovereignty is the birthright of each and all. It is on this basis that Stanton makes her case for the equality of women in every aspect of life. Her case is irrefutable.

Postscript: *The Woman's Bible* and *The Solitude of Self* are available in affordable paperback editions. Consult your local bookshop.

Second Postscript: The social purpose of Genesis 2:5-3:24, to warrant the subordination of women, is unmistakable. Yet, its author, evidently a man, was a poet of high literary talent, who gave classic expression to male desires, among them not only a will to dominate, but also a longing for union (to become one flesh), and admiration, even respect: the name "Eve" is a play on the verb "to live", and Eve is "the mother of all that lives".

Theodore Roosevelt's Progressivism

LIKE POPULISM, THE PROGRESSIVE MOVEMENT was embodied by a great personage, Theodore Roosevelt (1858–1919). He embodied in the way he lived, and he expressed it repeatedly in words, for example, in an address delivered in Chicago, in April 1899, two years before he became President, entitled "The Strenuous Life". The title says it all, but these words spell it out:

> In the last analysis a healthy nation can exist only when the men and women who make it up lead clean, vigorous, healthy lives; when their children are so trained that they shall endeavor, not to shirk difficulties, but to overcome them; not to seek ease, but to know how to wrest triumph from toil and risk. The man must be glad to do a man's work, to dare and endure and to labor; to keep himself, and to keep those dependent upon him. The woman must be the housewife, the helpmeet of the homemaker, the wise and fearless mother of many healthy children.

Theodore Roosevelt adhered to traditional gender roles. Yet, on reflection, the intended hierarchy may be inverted. Men labor with their bodies, but women's bodies surpass the power of men, for they can do things that men cannot: conceive and bear children, nurse them, and care for them with mother love. There is no greater love. I offer this as a proper interpretation of TR's meaning. But I digress.

Afflicted with severe asthma as a child, he overcame this disability through body building: weightlifting and boxing. He endured tragedy. In 1884, his wife died from complications due to childbirth; his mother died earlier on the same day. Grief stricken, TR went west to the Dakotas, and became a cowboy; there he breathed in the frontier spirit, which he put into words in a multi-volume work entitled, *The Winning of the West*, which anticipated Frederick Jackson Turner's frontier thesis (see Page 258). When the Spanish American War broke out, TR was serving as Assistant Secretary of the Navy. He resigned his post, and joined a newly formed cavalry regiment, dubbed the Rough Riders, of which he subsequently became head, and which he led to glory at the battle of San Juan Hill.

His children regarded him as a lion; and he is the namesake of the Teddy Bear. He possessed enormous energy, a strong will, great courage, and high intelligence.

What has this all to do with progressivism? It is important to keep in mind that the Progressive movement of the early 20th century had little if anything to do with 21st century Progressivism. Theodore Roosevelt envisioned the heroes of the Progressive Movement as a curious combination of the cowboy, the titan of industry, and the well-born elitist. His vision of America was of a nation's whose destiny was to gain supremacy in industrial and commercial growth throughout the world. And in military might as well. He was not a militarist, but, as the historian Richard Slotkin has shown, his Social Darwinian view of history involved the upward struggle if the nations and their people, and so it required a readiness to exert power. His political counsel, "Speak softly and carry a big stick", became a national motto.

While a student, Roosevelt came under the influence of Louis Agassiz (1807–73), who was founder of the Lawrence School of Science at Harvard. I will write more on Agassiz in a later essay; here it is important to note that Agassiz was the author and promoter of a dubious scientific theory concerning the races of mankind that gave credence to the prevailing racism. Racial identity was an essential part of personality development and a constant companion of the person. Roosevelt swallowed it all and made it the basis of his theory of historical progress, which he imagined was coming to fruition in the historical progress of the United States.

What caused Roosevelt to seek instruction with Agassiz was a deep and enduring love of nature. He studied natural history, became a naturalist and an environmentalist and conservationist. As president, he created four national parks, and gave strong support to the National Park Service. A noble legacy.

In his opinion, the native peoples of America were an unproductive race. Their eventual subjection and extermination were therefore inevitable in the march of history. They were succeeded by heroic figures, exemplified by Daniel Boone and Davy Crockett, who mastered the ways of the Indian, became bold hunters, but used their skills for a greater purpose, but above all they bequeathed to posterity the essential virtues of self-reliance. They and others like them opened pathways to the West, and many followed, these were the pioneers, in search of free land and with a will to make it productive. This was not the agrarian vision of Jefferson, who envisioned a nation of small farmers, not cowboys and their successors, the titans of industry--another role that Roosevelt championed. Not theirs, but the large industrial farms were what he favored, which was just one step on the way to this nation becoming an industrial and commercial giant. And, in the progress of America, just as farmers displaced cowboys, so agribusiness displaced farming with a requisite change of personnel, and they were accompanied by the great bankers and owners of great industries, who tended to come from the Eastern elite to whom Roosevelt belonged. To achieve this, Roosevelt saw it necessary that the government facilitate the growth of business, and he created the Department of Commerce in 1903. Like his cousin, Franklin, he believed that government must actively promote the economic growth of the nation. He believed this also with respect to conserving the environment.

Overall, Theodore Roosevelt's vision of America was imperial, and he likened it to ancient Rome. He was a strong advocate of the war with Spain in 1898, for it not only brought that empire to an end, but also secured American colonial expansion, a great step forward for Anglo-Saxon peoples.

Postscript: Theodore Roosevelt became President in September 1901, when President William McKinley was assassinated. He was reelected in 1904, and left office in January 1909, having pledged not to seek another term. Angered by the policies of his hand-picked successor, William Howard Taft, he left the Republican party and ran again for President under the banner of the newly formed Bull Moose Party. He was defeated by Woodrow Wilson. *"Bully for Teddy!"*

Racism and Science

RACISM IS A PREJUDICE, AND PREJUDICES ARE antithetical to truth. Therefore, the expression "scientific racism" is a contradiction of terms. This should be self-evident. Hence, it is disheartening to learn that scientific racism flourished in the United States, at Harvard University. In 1847 the university created the Lawrence School of Science with a gift of $50,000--at the time a very substantial amount, and named it after its donor, Abbott Lawrence, a wealthy industrialist and philanthropist. It was the first institution in the nation dedicated to pure research, to pure science, the search for truth for truth's sake. Louis Agassiz (1807-73) was appointed its first head.

Agassiz was a native of Switzerland, the son of a Protestant minister and a descendent of French Protestants, who, led by John Calvin, took refuge in Switzerland during the Reformation. He was richly gifted, physically, intellectually, socially, and economically. He was an imposing figure, his manner imperious, his energy enormous, his learning vast, his memory prodigious; he was outgoing and engaging, and wondrously articulate. In addition to all these advantages, he was a tireless self-promotor, and he used all his gifts in pursuit of this end.

As a student, he took advanced degrees in Germany in Medicine and Zoology. He also studied Geology, and from his research, he hypothesized that the earth had undergone a great ice age that caused the extinction of all life; it won him international fame. His interest in the ancient history of the earth led him into paleontology, the study of the most ancient forms of life, and in this endeavor, he was constantly in search of fossils and acquired a vast collection.

When Agassiz first came to the United States, he travelled to Philadelphia to confer with Samuel Morton, a physician and natural historian. Morton had acquired a large collection of human skulls, and from these and other human remains (he travelled to Egypt to inspect mummies) he concluded that there is more than one kind of human species. Therefore, God must have created mankind not once but several times; four to be precise, based on fossil evidence. His theory became known as Polygenism. He was condemned for contradicting the Bible, but he stood steadfast because of what he judged to be incontrovertible scientific evidence. A comparative study of skulls led him to conclude that the races differed in intellectual capacity. He based this on the different size of the skulls, and therefore, he inferred, of the brains they once contained. The brain, after all, is the seat of intelligence. He became convinced that God did not create all men equal. The signers of the Declaration of Independence were mistaken.

Agassiz embraced Morton's theory and brought it with him to Harvard. Polygenism acquired the status of a dogma. It should be noted that Agassiz, like Morton, was a creationist. This was before Darwin published *The Origin of Species (1859)*. When it appeared, Agassiz dismissed it with contempt. He remained to the end a creationist. It was as though his mind had become fossilized.

There was another side of Agassiz's racism. Until he arrived in America, he had never seen a person of African descent. In a letter to his mother, he described his first impression.

> "I experienced pity at the sight of this degraded and degenerate race. ... It is impossible for me to repress the feeling that they are not of the same blood as us. In seeing their black faces with their thick lips and grimacing teeth, the wool on their head, their bent knees, their elongated hands, their curved nails, and especially the livid color of the palms of their hands, I could not take my eyes off their faces in order to tell them to stay far away. And when they advanced that hideous hand towards my plate in order to serve me, I wished I were able to depart in order to eat a piece of bread elsewhere, rather than to dine with such service. What unhappiness

> for the white race? to have tied their
> existence so closely with that of Negroes
> in certain countries! God preserve us from
> such a contact!"

In any case, when Agassiz arrived at Harvard, armed with Morton's Polygenism, he brought his racism with him. He did not feel out of place. Nor did he hear any objections from his colleagues or students. To his credit, he expressed his hatred of the institution of slavery, and became an abolitionist, and, although his theory was well received in the South, he took no pride in that. He continued to modify his theory, doubling Morton's number of races to include Caucasian, Arctic, Mongol, American Indian, Negro, Hottentot, Malay, and Australian. He remained a tireless collector of fossils and founded the Harvard Museum of Comparative Zoology to house his collection.

He was a popular teacher. William James (1842-1910), who studied with him, concluded early on that most of what he said was humbug, yet he found him irresistible and his classes memorable by force of personality.

In fact, Agassiz's theory of natural history was more theology than science, with a large amount of ideology thrown into the mixture, the fossil evidence notwithstanding. Why God would have wanted to create mankind several times is puzzling. Although for Agassiz and Morton, and a host of other Europeans, statesmen and philosophers, the meaning was clear. God intended that among the races, there was one, endowed with superior intelligence and manliness, a super race of mortals, created to rule the rest. It fit well with European colonialism and with delusions of White supremacism.

Agassiz's legacy consists of lessons that must be unlearned.

Postscript: It is important to distinguish Social Darwinism from Darwin's theory of Evolution. The former is a racist doctrine rooted in ideology and myth; the latter is a biological theory based on empirical research. Darwin summarized his theory with the expression "descent with modification"; it concerns heredity and the origin of species, not of races, and it involves a process driven not by intelligent design but by chance and necessity. Darwin was a biologist, not a social philosopher. Like most of his contemporaries, he was afflicted with racial prejudice, but this did not cause him to confuse private opinion with impartial science.

VICTOR NUOVO

WAR AND PEACE

Woodrow Wilson

WOODROW WILSON (1826-1924) WAS ELECTED President of the United State in 1912. It was a moment of triumph for the Progressive movement, and it brought a sea change in the two-party system. Hitherto, the Republican party was the party of progressive causes, whilst the Democratic party tended toward conservative goals, especially social ones. In the deep south, the old Democrats persisted well into the 20th century, until mid-century, when Southern conservatives bolted the Democratic party and became Dixiecrats. They subsequently became Republicans.

The change was also facilitated by Theodore Roosevelt when he renounced the Republican Party and formed the Bull Moose Progressive Party. He did this, because his hand-picked successor to the presidency, William Howard Taft, had grown too conservative to his liking. In his bid for reelection, Taft finished third in the race after Wilson and Roosevelt, winning only Utah and Vermont. When Republicans returned to power in 1920, their candidates were Warren Harding and Calvin Coolidge, who were conservatives.

Wilson entitled his political program "The new Freedom" and pursued a progressive agenda which included free trade and government reform of commercial and financial institutions; he also expressed a deep concern for the human cost of American industrial growth and pledged to address it. He moved to the left of Roosevelt and stole his progressive fire. From then on, the Democratic party would be the party of liberals and progressives, whilst the Republican party continued on its conservative path.

Yet Wilson was an unlikely progressive. A southerner by birth and heritage, sympathetic to the lost cause of the confederacy, he was deeply religious and conservative by disposition. He was also afflicted with the American malady of racism, which caused him to see no wrong in pursuing a policy of racial segregation in the institutions of government, an ignoble legacy.

He did not set out on a career in politics. He first pursued a career in scholarship. In 1883 he entered Johns Hopkins University as a candidate for the Ph.D. Johns Hopkins had been founded only seven years previously primarily as a research university and was modelled on the model of German Universities. He took his degree in 1886 and began his academic career teaching political science. His specialty was the offices, institutions, and powers of civil government. In 1890, following appointments at Bryn Mawr College and Wesleyan University, he was appointed professor of jurisprudence and political economy at Princeton University. In Princeton, he found his intellectual and spiritual home. In 1902, he became President of the university. His reputation of excellence as a teacher, scholar, and reformer of higher education was spread far and wide.

His political rise was and meteoric. In 1910, he was elected governor of New Jersey. Two years later, he was elected President of the United States. This was no accident. Wilson arranged it himself, with the assistance of seasoned political operators, who aided him but never managed him. He was guided by his own lights and propelled by his strong will. No President, before or after, entered office better informed of the institutions of government and better equipped to use them effectively. The achievements of his first term (1913–17) remain unrivalled and will be treated in this essay. The tragic end of his second term (1917–21) and events that led to it will be the theme of the next essay.

Notwithstanding his racial prejudice, Wilson was a person of high moral principle and great moral courage. He was like Lincoln in this respect. It was the key to his success. Like Aristotle he regarded political theory as a continuation of ethics, and political practice as essentially moral and subject to moral rules. Party bosses and the moneyed interests of bankers and industrialists were to be resisted at every turn. As a politician, he endeavored to be true to his word, political promises were sacrosanct; they must never be idly made, and never be broken. It goes without saying, he was never boastful, and his public remarks were entirely free of malicious taunts, as I suspect his private ones were also. He was a man of consistent character. The contrast between Wilson and Donald

Trump is exceeds the difference between day and night, light and darkness.

What did he accomplish? In his first inaugural, Wilson called attention to the great social cost of American economic and industrial growth. These were costs paid by the laboring class: cruel working conditions, minimal wages, and their social and health consequences. He successfully introduced legislation establishing the eight-hour day. The first child labor laws were enacted during his first term; they prohibited the sale of products and materials whose production involved the labor of children, and in this connection, created the Federal Trade Commission. Under his leadership laws were enacted establishing the rights of labor against industry, thus empowering the rising labor movement. He introduced the graduated federal income tax. He created the Federal Reserve Bank as a means to regulate the interests of private bankers. And he sponsored a series of anti-trust laws to counteract the growing power of industrial conglomerates.

All of these achievements led to the enlargement of government and the increase of it its power. Unlike his fellow Progressive, Theodore Roosevelt, Wilson's scruples made him reluctant to proceed too forcefully in this direction. He feared the abuse of power. He was, after all, reared by Calvinists, and believed in original sin; he was sure of the truth articulated by Lord Acton, that "power tends to corrupt, and absolute power corrupts absolutely". He especially feared the abuse of executive power. He never tired of reminding his audiences that the founding of this nation was a political response to the tyranny of the British monarch. To achieve his ends, he relied on the power of speech to persuade. In this capability, he was well gifted, and, for a time, remarkably successful.

Postscript: In preparing this essay, I have relied on an excellent collection of Wilson's writings: *Woodrow Wilson: Essential Writings and Speeches of the Scholar-President*, edited by Mario DiNunzio, which includes an informative introduction. Consult your local bookshop.

The Great War

T HE FIRST WORLD WAR (1914-18), a.k.a. The Great War, was an epochal moment in world history. It brought the long 19th century to an end and marked the beginning of the 20th. It wrote *finis* to the Gilded Age and its sanguine optimism. Its political and economic effects were felt throughout the remainder of the century and they continue even today. In this respect, we are still living in an even longer 20th century. War or the threat of war have persisted from then until now, as have most of the social and economic ills which followed in its train. It caused the Great Depression, Totalitarianism, the Second World War, and its aftermath.

And yet it was a most unlikely war. In 1910, a British journalist, Norman Angell published a book entitled *The Great Illusion*. Theme of the book was the unlikelihood of war among European nations. In the aftermath of the war, Angell and his book were dismissed with scorn by many. But more sympathetic readers have countered that this is because his critics missed Angell's irony and the subtlety of his argument. His theme was not a thesis; he did not argue that war was unlikely, but that, for their best interests, national leaders *must consider* it unlikely. He argued that because of the commercial and economic interdependence of the nations of Europe, Europe had become a community with shared interests; there was no need for separate nations to possess standing armies to defend themselves against their neighbors, nor was there need for them to seek an increase of territory at their neighbors' expense, for their destinies had become intertwined.

Europe had become a vibrant economic community; therefore, for European nations to make war against each other would be suicidal. He concluded that it would be irrational for any European nation to make aggressive war against its neighbors, and that wars of self defense were therefore unnecessary as were the building up of great standing armies. It was a sound argument then, and it remains so today, one well worth retrieving and directing against proponents of the new nationalism and militarism. It follows that the so-called

Great War was a tragic absurdity. The most difficult task for historians of the First World War has been to explain why it happened.

The war was the chief cause of the change in the character of Woodrow Wilson's presidency from triumph to tragedy.

Wilson's first response to the war was to keep America out of it, and to maintain a strict neutrality towards the belligerents. These were the *Central Powers*, consisting of Austria-Hungary, Germany, Bulgaria, and the Ottoman Empire, and the *Triple Alliance*, or the *Entente* or *Allies* for short, comprising France, Russia, and the United Kingdom. His chief aim was peace, and it remained his abiding hope. He offered himself to the warring parties as an impartial mediator. His concern went well beyond persuading them to meet and settle their differences. His goal was a durable peace among all nations, the end of war and the threat of war, and to achieve this, it was necessary to create a supra-national institution to enforce peace, a league of nations endowed with superior force.

> "It will be absolutely necessary that a force be created as a guarantor of the permanency of the settlement so much greater than the any nation ... or any alliance [of nations] ... If the peace to be made is to endure, it must be a peace made secure by the organized major force of mankind"

The force he intended was not military, but the rule of law, much as our Constitution is sovereign over states. It required an international covenant of peoples.

Wilson was following in the footsteps of Thomas Hobbes. He imagined the current international condition to be "a state of nature", a state of war of all against all, which could be ended by acknowledging a superior power guided by law, a law of nature that prescribed "Make peace and keep it."

He met with no success. And Germany challenged his impartiality beyond all rational limits. The German U-boat campaign against trans-Atlantic shipping caused the loss of American lives. Then there was the notorious Zimmerman affair, in which Germany, foreseeing American entry into the war, tried to induce Mexico to declare war against the United States, promising as a reward the return of territories lost in the Mexican War: Texas, Arizona, and New Mexico. On April 2, 1918, Wilson asked Congress to declare war, and the United States joined the Allies. "And the war came."

Yet Wilson did not forget his plan; he expanded and refined it. When the war ended, he led the American delegation to the Paris Peace Conference, convened in January 1919. Among the goals he sought were the restoration of territories lost during the war; guarantees of autonomy to all nations; free trade; and a League of Nations, open to all nations. He resisted, in vain, the demands of France and Britain to punish Germany, and although agreement was reached to create a League of Nations, its powers were not as great as he desired.

When he returned to the United States, he was met with strong opposition to the League. His chief opponent was Senator Henry Cabot Lodge; another was Theodore Roosevelt. The issue was sovereignty, and it pitted nationalists against internationalists. Nationalists contended that membership in the League would limit the sovereignty of nations. Internationalists did not deny this but contended that it was necessary to create a lasting peace. It was the only means to end chronic war.

Wilson went on a nationwide campaign for American entry into the League. His effort failed as did his health. He suffered a stroke, and returned to Washington; thereafter he was dependent on others to perform the duties of his office until his term ended in March, 1921.

Postscript: The Great Illusion is available online @ gutenberg.org. In 1931, Norman Angell was knighted, and in 1933 he was awarded the Nobel Peace Prize. Key writings by Wilson are provided in *Woodrow Wilson: Essential Writings and Speeches of the Scholar-President,* edited by Mario DiNunzio. Also, the 1944 film, *Wilson,* starring Alexander Knox in the title role, is well worth watching.

VICTOR NUOVO

Herbert Hoover and the Great Depression

THE GREAT DEPRESSION WAS AN INTERNATIONAL economic catastrophe that lasted for a decade, 1929–1939. Its end came because of a second world catastrophe that caused a burst of industrial development and employment, a second Great War, in which 75 million died, two-thirds of them civilians, many of them victims of genocide. It was a high price to pay for full employment.

None of this was foreseen in 1928, when Herbert Clark Hoover (1874–1964) was elected the 31st President of the United States, succeeding the lackluster Calvin Coolidge. He won by a landslide, winning sixty percent of the popular vote, forty of the then forty-eight states, and receiving 444 electoral votes, almost five times the number won by his Democratic opponent, Alfred E. Smith.

He entered office with a record of outstanding public service. During first World War and its aftermath he headed up a commission to provide food and relief to Belgium and other European nations ravaged by the war, and he carried out his duties with efficiency and compassion. During the Harding and Coolidge administrations, he served as Secretary of Commerce with distinction, an odd man out in an otherwise very undistinguished and corrupt administration; his reputation as a Progressive was well deserved. Like Wilson, he worried over the ill effects of industrial growth on the working class and the social effects of income inequality.

Born in Iowa, into a Quaker family, of humble origins, he was a "scion of the common man"; Aaron Copland's fanfare is a fitting accompaniment to his early life. Orphaned in early childhood, he had little formal education; in 1885 he went to live with his uncle, a physician in Oregon, whose only son had died the year before. In 1891 he was admitted to Stanford University, where he studied geology and trained to become a mining engineer. After graduation, he found employment with a British mining company, eventually becoming a partner. He gained an international reputation as an expert on mining techniques and metallurgy, and for his expertise in managing large, complex industrial processes. He wrote what became the standard textbook on mining practices. From all of this, he acquired a great fortune and world reputation as a principled technocrat.

He was also a political philosopher; he lectured at Stanford and Columbia. In 1922 he published *American Individualism*, which provides a clear, concise summary of his thinking, and a classic expression of what has come to be known as American exceptionalism.

Hoover wrote that what distinguishes this nation from all other nations of the world, that is, what makes it exceptional, is American individualism. He observed that ever since the Enlightenment, individualism had become the ruling principle of European society. However, European individualism was selfish; its rule was: "every man for himself and the devil take the hindmost". He contended that European nations based their foreign policies on it, and that it was the ideological cause of the Great War and the vengeful peace that followed it, which created resentment and fueled cruel political fantasies, perhaps crueler in their consequences than any the world had ever seen.

However, Hoover wrote, American individualism is radically different. It is based on the premise that every individual is obliged to serve others, to strive for the common good. Service to others was for him the first rule of the moral life of individuals, and through them of government, and of every public institution. He labelled his doctrine "progressive individualism", and it did indeed have a progressive ring to it: it required complete social equality, a classless society; universal education; equal opportunity and the promise to provide the means to all to develop to the fullest their native capacities, and to live by the dignity of their accomplishments. His presidential campaign even had progressive slogan: "a chicken in every pot".

And yet, in spite of his progressive agenda, four years later, in his bid for reelection, Hoover was defeated by an even greater majority than what he had attained in 1928. Why did this happen? No doubt, many voters believed that the Great Depression, which began with the Stock Market Crash six months after he took office, was his fault. But that was not so. More likely it was due to a loss of confidence is his ability to deal with the crises that followed, despite his record of bringing food and relief to war ravaged Europe.

The usual explanation is that Hoover looked with disfavor on direct government action, preferring to rely instead on the voluntary efforts of private initiative to reverse the downward course of the economy; but it was not forthcoming. He did propose that government initiate programs of public works--one instance of this is the construction of Hoover Dam, begun in 1931, but he left it largely up to the states to implement these programs and to find the means to pay for it. One obstacle in his way may have been his very principle of individualism, which demanded of every citizen a large measure of self reliance, and which made him reluctant to provide direct relief to individuals, despite the hard times they endured.

After he left office, Hoover did not abandon his principles or his capability, or his desire to render some public service. In 1946, President Truman sent Hoover to Germany to recommend measures to provide food and relief, and measures for the reconstruction of Germany; a year later, Truman appointed Hoover to a commission, which came to be known as the Hoover Commission after he was elected chair, to make recommendations for a complete reorganization of the executive branch of government. He performed these duties with his usual competence.

Yet, reading his memoirs, one feels that his political defeat left him deeply saddened and resentful, and one cannot help but feel his pain. It must be said that no man displayed the character of an American conservative better than he; this may be his legacy.

Postscript: Hoover's *American Individualism* is available in a paperback edition and is worth reading. In preparing this essay, I have relied on *The American People in the Great Depression*, by David M. Kennedy, and John Kenneth Galbraith, *The Great Crash, 1929*, both in paperback. Consult your local bookshop.

FDR and the New Deal

THE ELECTION OF FRANKLIN DELANO ROOSEVELT (1882-1945) to the presidency in 1932 marks a decisive turning point in this nation's history. The policies he put into practice during the first term of his administration changed the character of the nation, from one whose economic and social fortunes were directed by unregulated, *laissez faire* capitalism, by the self-serving exploits of economic adventurers, a.k.a, "robber barons" and their ilk, to a social democracy in which government assumed a prominent role in regulating industrial and financial practices, providing jobs for the unemployed, and protecting its citizens from harm caused by capitalist misadventures that were inimical to the public good. The Federal government became the chief protector of its citizens, and the guarantor of their social security. In the end, the New Deal, which was the name Roosevelt gave to his program of economic recovery, did not accomplish all of its goals completely; but it redefined the nation's destiny, which, notwithstanding many reverses, is still on the horizon, a promise that always beckons, and which may in future deliver this nation from the new dark age in which we have fallen.

Roosevelt's accomplishments, during the depression and the war that followed, are all the more remarkable, given the physical handicap he had to overcome to achieve them. In his youth and early manhood, he was well favored and well endowed. He was a born aristocrat, member of distinguished family, of great wealth, and educated at Harvard and Columbia Law School. Frances Perkins (1882-1965), who would later serve as his secretary of labor for thirteen years-- the first woman to serve as a cabinet secretary, and who knew him socially, described the young Franklin as "a supercilious snob, who really didn't seem to like people very much." In coming years, this attitude would reverse itself, and this once proud aristocrat became the common man's best friend, motivated by a powerful political ambition coupled with a genuine and captivating friendliness.

In 1907, Roosevelt passed the bar exam, and left law school without completing his studies. He practiced law for a while, but his real interest was not in business but politics. In 1911 he was elected to the New York State Senate, where he gained a reputation as a reformer, a champion of progressive policies, and a formidable enemy of political bosses. Reelected for a second term, he resigned his seat in order to accept Woodrow Wilson's appointment as assistant secretary of the Navy, where he remained until Wilson left office in 1920. In the same year, at the Democratic national convention, he received the vice-presidential nomination, and ran unsuccessfully with James M. Cox, the presidential nominee, against the Republican duo of Warren Harding and Calvin Coolidge. Not long after, he was stricken with polio. He became paralyzed from the waste down and spent the next eight years in rehabilitation and planning for his future. In 1928 he was elected governor of New York; he was reelected in 1930 and set his eyes on the Presidency. Elected in 1932, he was reelected in 1936, 1940, and 1944, and died in office on April 12, 1945. He was 63 years old.

Just what was the New Deal? It was not a plan to restore the nation's economy, rather its purpose was to put people to work; Roosevelt called it "work relief". And he set about to achieve this through a massive program of public works. Two government agencies were created to achieve this: the Public Works Administration. (PWA) and the Works Progress Administration (WPA). The former provided loans and grants to states to engage in public works projects; the latter provided employment through the construction of public buildings: schools, hospitals, libraries, post-offices, court houses, and suchlike, along with roads, bridges, and water and sewer lines, and it brought about the electrification of rural areas. It also gave support to the creative and performing arts through the Federal Art Project, the Federal Music Project, the Federal Theatre Project, and the Federal Writers' Project. These programs not only provided jobs for artists and writers but produced a cultural renaissance.

Historians have noted that, in spite of the extraordinary measures taken to remedy the grave effects of the Great Depression, the government of the United States came through it all safe and sound. Although there was no doubt the nation was in the midst of a national emergency of great magnitude and that strong executive leadership was needed to see it through, Roosevelt did not exceed the constitutional powers of the president to achieve them; during the first hundred days of his presidency, he called Congress in session and worked closely with it to provide new laws and authorize additional funds needed to meet the current crisis; the separation of powers remained secure; the Constitution unscathed; the rule of law prevailed. The great economist, John Maynard Keynes described Roosevelt's policies as "reasoned experiments within an existing social system." In this respect, Roosevelt stood apart from other national leaders: Adolf Hitler, Benito Mussolini, and Joseph Stalin, who justified their seizure of power and dictatorial methods as the only sure way to achieve the stability and renewal of their nations. They were mistaken, and the great cost of their mistakes is beyond all counting, and the horrors they caused, too painful to describe.

In planning and executing his program of social reform, Franklin Roosevelt could rely on the wise counsel and public example of his wife Eleanor Roosevelt (1884–1962). She was not only the longest serving First Lady, but she was also the first to use her position to political advantage in pursuit of social programs that went beyond those of the New Deal; she was a skilled communicator, indefatigable, highly principled, and fully capable to carry out the duties of President. Her deep compassion for ordinary people led Harry Truman to call her "The first Lady of the world". She became the moral conscience of America. More will follow in a subsequent essay.

FDR and the Second World War

THE SECOND WORLD WAR BEGAN ON September 1, 1939 and lasted for six years and a day. It ended on September 2, 1945, with the surrender of Japan; the German surrender happened four months earlier, on May 7, 1945, 25 days after the death of Franklin Roosevelt. Both nations surrendered unconditionally. It was a victory for Democracy.

When the war began, a good outcome seemed far from certain. On September 1, 1939, without declaring war, Germany invaded Poland and conquered it in less than a month. It then proceeded, with the Soviet Union, with which it had recently concluded a non-aggression pact, to dismember and divide up Poland. Then, after a lull of eight months, Germany let loose its forces on Western Europe, and in two months conquered Norway, Denmark, Luxembourg, Holland, Belgium, and France. In June 1941, a non-aggression pact notwithstanding, Germany invaded Russia with an enormous force. Hitler's purpose was genocidal, to annex the Western (European) portion of Russia, enslave its people, (that is those able to engage in hard labor–the remainder would be terminated), and repopulate it with German speaking, Aryan, peoples.

Japan began its territorial conquests almost a decade earlier, with the annexation of Manchuria. In 1937 it invaded China. In September 1940, it entered into a military alliance with Germany and Italy, the Tripartite Pact, and they named themselves "The Axis Powers" to signify that they expected the world soon to turn at their bidding. It was agreed that Japan would be free to make itself master of Asia, leaving Europe and Africa to Germany and Italy. Soon after Japan's forces overran much of Southeast Asia and threatened India.

Britain stood alone.

President Roosevelt, following Woodrow Wilson a generation before, pursued a policy of American neutrality. Having served in Wilson's administration, he remarked he had seen all this before, and he feared the outcome; he also felt obliged to prepare for it. Between 1935 and 1937, Congress passed three neutrality acts, which Roosevelt signed, prohibiting the sale of arms manufactured in the US to any belligerent nation and prohibiting US naval vessels from entering any war zone. During his campaign for reelection in 1940, Roosevelt pledged that this nation would not declare war against either of the Axis Powers (German, Italy, and Japan) unless attacked. Yet it was evident which side he favored, and, despite the neutrality laws, he contrived ways to provide the British with the arms and materiel they desperately needed. His policies of "Cash and Carry" and "Lend Lease" were cleverly designed to circumvent the law. His invitation to George VI and

Queen Mary to visit the United States was further evidence of his favoritism.

What followed is well known. On December 7, 1941, Japan attacked Pearl Harbor. Four days later, on December 11, Germany and Italy declared war against the United States. The nation was once again at war.

Roosevelt's critics have argued that the Japanese attack came as no surprise to him, because he deliberately provoked it. The charge is baseless, and I will say no more of it. Nonetheless, in retrospect, gathering the Pacific Fleet at Pearl Harbor was a serious miscalculation. Roosevelt saw it as a deterrent; the Japanese saw it as an opportunity. Its preemptive attack took place without a declaration of war; in fact, the Japanese Ambassador and the Secretary of State were at the time engaged in negotiations as a means of avoiding war.

The reasons for Roosevelt's favoritism are easy to discern. Adolf Hitler had provided the world with a look into the soul of absolute evil, driven by racial hatred, full of mad and murderous fantasies, which would be carried out by his minions with exquisite cruelty and consummate efficiency. Japan and Italy followed suit. Great Britain not only stood alone, it stood for Democracy against Totalitarianism. How could he not favor her?

After Pearl Harbor, in early 1942, Roosevelt acknowledged that the possibility that the United States and Britain might lose the war was real. Hollywood captured that sense of inevitable loss in its film "Bataan", where the only recourse was heroic defiance and death. It was not until the Battle of Midway, June 4–6, 1942, that the prospect changed, and there was hope for victory. From then on, the Allies and the Axis Powers were engaged in total war.

Roosevelt spent himself in the effort to achieve total victory over the Axis Powers, and, through his leadership, and the heroic effort and sacrifices of innumerable others, it was finally achieved. But he did not live to see it. He died on April 12, 1945. The cause of death was a cerebral hemorrhage. I remember the day.

Postscript: Besides his failure to anticipate the Japanese attack on Pearl Harbor, Roosevelt has also been justly criticized on two further counts: first, his failure to take seriously Hitler's antisemitism and to act to prevent or mitigate his genocidal practices, and his policy of internment of Japanese Americans.

Postscript 2: I append another personal remembrance. Until I was 13 years old, I knew only one President, FDR. His presence filled my childhood and my youth. The events that I have described fill my memory. He is the only President that I have ever seen in the flesh. When King George VI and Queen Mary made their state visit to the United States in June 1939, they visited the New York World's Fair. Standing on a highway bridge overlooking Long Island's Grand Central Parkway, I watched the King and Queen drive past in an open car, accompanied by Franklin and Eleanor, on their way to the Fair. They were smiling and waving regally. I remember it well.

Elusive Peace

HISTORIANS HAVE JUDGED WORLD WAR II to be the most destructive war in human history. Seventy-five million persons died, two-thirds of them civilians. One of the causes of so many civilian deaths was the aerial bombing of urban and industrial centers, another was the genocidal murder of six-million Jews and innumerable others whom Hitler, in his diabolical delusions, judged unworthy of existence; finally, the killing power of weapons was increased exponentially–weapons of mass destruction were invented capable of obliterating entire cities in a single blast. It has been reported that shortly after the war ended, Albert Einstein was asked what weapons might be used in World War III, if it should ever occur; he responded that he did not know what weapons would be used in a third world war, but he was certain that "World War IV will be fought with sticks and stones". It was a sober warning.

And yet, from 1945 until the present, the United States has been continually at war or engaged in military interventions or standoffs: Korea, Vietnam, Cuba, Grenada, Panama, the Persian Gulf, Bosnia, Afghanistan, Libya, Iraq, Syria, and Yemen. To be sure, these were more or less local conflicts, not worldwide conflagrations, yet each was a test of the power and influence of the great powers. Reinhold Niebuhr summed up the situation as "a balance of terror".

Peace of a sort was maintained between the United States and the Soviet Union until the latter's downfall. Since then, China has emerged as this nation's chief rival in the continuing international game of power politics. Meanwhile Russia waits in the wings, aspiring once again to become a major player, while most other nations stand ready on the sidelines, as if military preparedness were the only way to maintain the peace, a tribute to the motto, "Don't tread on me". But is this really peace, or is it just a pause or time out in a chronic state of war?

Why is peace so elusive? Thomas Hobbes had a ready answer to this question: Because human beings are by nature aggressive and combative animals, and in their natural state, they tend to be at war with one another. His remedy was the creation of civil societies endowed with power to keep the peace, by force if necessary. But is this sufficient? Or are civil states merely oases in a sea of war, a.k.a. the "state of nature"? As John Locke observed, the creation of civil societies or nation states merely relocates the "state of nature" beyond national borders, where it lurks in the wasteland between nations, ready to pounce. Hence, war or the rumor of war remains an ever-present threat, like a deadly virus. The volatile relations between European states during the 18th, 19th, and 20th centuries confirm this.

But this is too general an answer to the question, and hence it is inadequate, even if it is true, which I believe it is. Hobbes' sole purpose in writing about these things was to create peace. For him, the supreme law of nature and of politics is "Make peace and keep it!" So the question remains, "Why is peace so elusive?" Or more concretely: Why have human nations been unable to create a lasting peace among themselves in spite of the horror and lasting pain of war? A lasting peace was what Woodrow Wilson aimed for following the first World War, and it was Franklin Roosevelt's hope to follow the second; it led to the founding of the United Nations and other international agencies devoted to peace and reconciliation. Why have these efforts not succeeded?

Walter Lippmann (1889–1974) had an answer that more closely fits the state of European public affairs in the 20th century. In a book he completed in 1937 but did not publish until 1943, he wrote that the Great world powers: Germany, Japan, and Russia, adopted total war as an international policy, as a deterrence rather than a practice, yet one that required constant military preparedness. The roots of total war were planted in antiquity. Rome waged total war against Carthage; its purpose was just not victory in battle in order to gain territory and tribute, but the total destruction of its enemy. Racial and ideological totalitarianisms found total war a practice well suited to its purposes; its most zealous practitioners were Adolf Hitler and Joseph Stalin. Winston Churchill promoted it.

In the 21st century, the likelihood of total war seems remote. Yet all the great powers, and many not so great, possess the means to wage it. And militarism is on the rise.

The wisdom of Hobbes resides in his recognition that warmakers must become peacemakers. He was a Realist, and he did not expect that peace would be accomplished by divine intervention. He regarded peacemaking as a matter of mere self interest. If you go to war against your neighbor, it is a toss-up who will win in the end. Only a vain and impulsive fool would be confident of the outcome. Not to mention that violence breeds violence, and once the killing begins, Armageddon is sure to follow. Hobbes wisdom is not pretty, but it is wise and unsentimental–vintage worldly wisdom.

Postscript: Thomas Hobbes' *Leviathan* is available in an Oxford paperback; Walter Lippmann's writings are not easy to find. His two most important works: *The Good Society* and *The Public Philosophy* are available only by print on demand. A Lippmann revival is overdue. In the meantime, visit your local library.

Franklin Roosevelt's Women

Franklin Roosevelt delighted in the company of women, and when he died suddenly on April 12, 1945, he was surrounded by them. His wife Eleanor Roosevelt (1884-1962) was not among them. She was out and about attending to her own affairs. Although she took her duties as First Lady very seriously and performed them with efficiency and grace, and never failed to give her husband constant support and wise counsel, she had other pots to boil beside presidential ones, and, by her own efforts, she rose to international prominence, indeed greatness.

Her husband's philandering, which she painfully discovered early in their marriage, was a principal cause of her independence. But the sources of her greatness lay in herself alone. She was another Abigail Adams, but freer and more productive. She was a person of the highest moral seriousness and integrity, an intellectual, a prolific author, a leading feminist, and she strode upon the world stage with unquestioned authority. Among her intellectual friends was the theologian Reinhold Niebuhr, and she paid visits to Union Theological Seminary in New York to consult with him. I saw her there several times, and heard her speak, and I cherish those memories.

But Franklin Roosevelt not only enjoyed the company of women, but he also depended on them. Chief among them was his mother, Sara Delano Roosevelt (1854–1941). Eleanor, with whom he fell in love and married, was another. Still another was Lucy Mercer (1894–1948). In 1914, she became Eleanor's social secretary and a member of the household. From all accounts, she was "lovely to look at, delightful to know, and heaven to kiss", and she was conveniently nearby.

After the birth of their fifth child, Eleanor and Franklin moved to a larger house with separate bedrooms. The stage was set.

There is no record of when Franklin and Lucy became lovers. Eleanor discovered it while unpacking Franklin's suitcase, after his return from a trip from Europe in 1918. She found a packet of letters, love letters between Franklin and Lucy. Confronted with the damaging evidence, Franklin admitted his wrongdoing. Eleanor destroyed the letters. Lucy was dismissed.

Franklin offered Eleanor a divorce. She was willing. She had no taste for erotic living, and she blamed herself for not providing her husband with all that he needed. Sara forbad it and told Franklin that if he divorced Eleanor, she would cut him off without a cent. In the end, Franklin promised never to see Lucy again. It was a promise he would not keep. Lucy was with him when he died and there were other meetings in between.

By offering her a divorce, Franklin must have been aware that he would also have to resign his position as Assistant Secretary of the Navy or be dismissed, and that this would end his political career. Like Edward Windsor, he may for a while have been willing to sacrifice high office for the woman he loved. But he relented. Besides, greatness would have eluded him without Eleanor. Perhaps he realized this, for she was his better self, his conscience. And no person without a conscience can ever aspire to greatness. It follows that Eleanor Roosevelt was a major source of her husband's greatness. It lay in her moral seriousness and intellectual daring, which, joined with Franklin's mastery of the art of politics became an irresistible force.

Nature also played its part. In 1921 Franklin contracted poliomyelitis, which left him a paraplegic. Eleanor nursed him, and for a while their intimacy was restored. Those close to him observed that his affliction caused a change in his personality: he became a more caring person. Sara preferred that Franklin should abandon political ambition and live out his days in Hyde Park, guarded by women. But Franklin remained "master of his fate" and planned his career. In 1928 he was elected governor of New York, and he was reelected in 1930. In 1932, he was elected president of the United States.

Eleanor Roosevelt achieved, or perhaps, declared her independence by becoming a writer. In 1933, she published her first book entitled *It's up to the Women*. The title is reminiscent of Abigail Adam's playful counsel to her husband during the constitutional convention, "I desire that you would remember the ladies". Mindful of the effects of the Great Depression, she wrote it to offer counsel to women, and to men also–any who would dare to read it. She stated her theme in words that seem relevant today:

> "The present crisis [the Great Depression] is different from all the others, but it is, after all a kind of warfare against an intangible enemy of want and depression rather than a physical force. And I hold it equally true that in this present crisis it is going to be the women who will tip the scales and bring us safely out of it"

There follows an extended discourse giving advice and counsel on how to live in hard times. It is timely. There are echoes in it of Elizabeth Cady Stanton's *Solitude of Self*.

In 1935, Eleanor became a syndicated newspaper columnist, and wrote a daily column entitled "My Day". She continued writing until 1962, the year she died. Reading her columns today provides insight into the great crises of the middle of the century: depression, war, segregation, civil rights.

It is in the field of human rights that Eleanor Roosevelt has established her most lasting legacy. In 1945 President Truman appointed her a delegate to the United Nations General Assembly, and she became a member of its newly formed Civil Rights Commission. Its members elected her its Chair, and under her leadership, the committee crafted *The Universal Declaration of Human Rights*, adopted by the UN General Assembly in 1948. It declared that all persons possess the right to life, liberty, and person (i.e., the right to be oneself), and the right of equal protection under law; it condemned slavery, cruel and unusual punishment, and sanctioned revolution against tyranny and oppression. It was a universal declaration of independence. The member nations pledged "to secure universal recognition and observance" of these rights within their particular domains, and throughout the world. This was Eleanor Roosevelt's legacy; and by it she belongs to the ages.

But my story is not ended. There is another woman who figured importantly in Franklin Roosevelt's career.

Postscript: There is a convenient collection "My Day" edited by David Emblidge, *My Day*, MJF Books; Also see *The Autobiography of Eleanor Roosevelt*, Harper Perennial Paperback and *A World Made New*, by Mary Ann Glendon, which is tells the story of the making of *The Declaration of Human Rights*.

The Indomitable Frances Perkins

"FRANCIS PERKINS" IS NOT A HOUSEHOLD NAME, but it ought to be, for Frances Perkins herself (1880–1965) is legendary. The title of a recent biography *"The Woman Behind the New Deal"* doesn't say enough, for she conceived the New Deal, gave it birth, and nurtured it to maturity. In 1933, when Franklin Roosevelt was choosing his cabinet, he offered her the position of Secretary of Labor. She accepted and remained in office until 1945. She was the first woman to serve as a cabinet secretary, and she holds the record as the longest serving cabinet secretary in US history. It is a record not likely to be broken. But she did much more than serve time. Her agenda included the following: an eight-hour workday, a forty-hour workweek, time-and-a-half for overtime, minimum wage, workers compensation, unemployment insurance, child labor laws, and social security--all of them programs that in 1933 seemed radical but are now staples in a good society. She was also an early advocate of a national health insurance. The historian Adam Cohen ranks her with the American founders, for she began a revolution that is still ongoing.

Fannie Coralie Perkins was born in Boston and grew up in Worcester, Massachusetts. Her father, Frederick Perkins, a well educated, patrician, was not well endowed financially, and made a modest living for his family as a retailer of stationery and office supplies. He took a special interest in Fannie's education. He saw to it that she received a classical education, tutoring her in Greek while she was still a child and introducing her to the Classics. She attended Worcester Classical High School, where she studied Greek and Latin, and Mount Holyoke College, taking her bachelor's degree in chemistry and physics. Later in life, she studied economics as a graduate student at the Wharton School, and in 1910, she received a master's degree in political science from Columbia University.

When she was ten, she received a lesson of a different sort from her mother. Out shopping for a new outfit, her mother told her that she was not and never would be beautiful, and that she should dress accordingly. This did not cause her to forget that she was a woman. She resolved to become a strong woman, entirely self-possessed, and she devised ways to use her womanhood as an instrument of power to make her way in a man's world. She renamed herself "Frances"; she chose it because it was a stately name, and also because some men, not having met her, might suppose that she was a man, and would be unsettled on meeting her, to discover that they must deal with a woman. For the same reason, she chose a wardrobe that made her a appear matronly; it added to her power, for as a noted labor leader remarked, "every man has a mother". She was also a keen observer of men, and she recorded her observations in a notebook which she entitled *"Notes on the Male Mind"*. In her dealings with men, she was always armed with knowledge, proving Francis Bacon's assertion "Scientia potentia est", "Knowledge is power".

After college, she took a position as a teacher at a girl's school in Lake Forest Illinois, and became a volunteer at Hull House in Chicago, where she came under the influence of Jane Addams (1869–1935), founder of the settlement house movement in America. Settlement houses offered various services to poor, mostly immigrant families in the inner city, including lodging, child-care, instruction in English, job training. It was a place where upper-class, educated people with a social conscience could live side by side with the underprivileged. Her visits to Hull House caused Frances to change her vocation. She would become a social worker. She moved to Philadelphia to work for a charitable organization dedicated to investigating and exposing prostitution rings in the city. She became a socialist. In 1909 she moved to New York to continue her studies at Columbia University, where she had received a fellowship. There she met Robert Moses (1888–1981), who was destined to rebuild New York, and Sinclair Lewis (1885–1951), who proposed marriage. She also met Paul Caldwell Wilson (1876-1952), who shared her social and political interests, and whom she married in 1910. It was a happy marriage at first, they had a beautiful daughter, Susanna, but Paul began to show symptoms of bi-polar disorder. He was unable to work, was hospitalized, and finally committed to a sanatorium, where he spent most of the rest of his life. Frances became the family provider.

In New York, she became associated with Progressives, among them Theodore Roosevelt, but also with Democratic Reformers, among them Al Smith (1873–1944), Franklin Roosevelt, and John Mitchell (1870–1919), president of the United Mine Workers Union. who also proposed marriage; Mitchell was succeeded by John L. Lewis (1880–1969), whom she knew but did not fully trust. Al Smith was elected governor of New York in 1918, and he appointed her to a seat on the New York State Industrial Commission. Its purpose was to investigate workplace conditions and recommend improvements. She became not only an incisive investigator but a powerful lobbyist for labor reform. Ten years later, Franklin Roosevelt, then governor of New York, made her head of the Commission. He did so, because of her administrative skill, her compassion for the underprivileged and the working poor, and her indomitable will.

After his election to the presidency, Roosevelt appointed her Secretary of Labor. And she was tireless in promoting and implementing the social programs of the New Deal. In doing so, she was often in conflict with other members of Roosevelt's cabinet, all male, but she always could count on the President's support. When Roosevelt died, as was customary for cabinet officers, she offered her resignation to the new president, Harry Truman, which he accepted. He replaced her with a political crony unfit for the job, which infuriated Eleanor Roosevelt. He offered her other appointments in his administration, and she remained in government until 1952.

In need of employment, she received an invitation to teach at Cornell in its school of Labor and Industrial Relations. She accepted and remained to the end of her life. She lectured on politics and social policy. She also was appointed senior resident at Telluride House, a residential house for students and faculty; she was much beloved by students for her wit and wisdom, and for her motherly care. When she died, students at Telluride House were her pallbearers.

Postscript: Unfortunately, Perkins delivered her lectures extemporaneously, and no written record of them survives. However, her biography of Franklin Roosevelt, *The Roosevelt I Knew,* is also a memoir, perhaps the best ever written of the New Deal and of the man who presided over it. It is available in paperback, by Penguin. Consult your local bookseller.

VICTOR NUOVO

WHERE DO WE GO FROM HERE?

The New Frontier

"The New Frontier" was the keynote of John F. Kennedy's presidential campaign, which he sounded at the Democratic national convention in San Francisco on July 15, 1960, in a speech accepting the party's nomination to become President of the United States. He presented himself standing at the physical boundary of the continental United States looking west. In his mind's eye, inspired by the spirit of Frederick Jackson Turner, he imagined before him a vast wilderness filled with an array of challenges, and he called upon the people to gather with him at this new frontier, and to join him as he crossed over.

> "I stand tonight facing west on what was once the last frontier. From the lands that stretch three thousand miles behind me, the pioneers of old gave up their safety, their comfort and sometimes their lives to build a new world here in the West. ... Today some would say that those struggles are over–that all the horizons have been explored–that all the battles have been won–that there is no longer an American frontier....But I tell you the New Frontier

is here, whether we seek it or not. Beyond that frontier are the uncharted areas of science and space, unsolved problems of peace and war, unconquered pockets of ignorance and prejudice, unanswered questions of poverty and surplus. It would be easier to shrink back from that frontier, to look to the safe mediocrity of the past, to be lulled by good intentions and high rhetoric–and those who prefer that course should not cast their votes for me, regardless of party… I believe the times demand new invention, innovation, imagination, decision. I am asking each of you to be pioneers on that New Frontier. My call is to the young in heart, regardless of age–to all who respond to the Scriptural call: Be strong and of a good courage; be not afraid, neither be thou dismayed."

Counterfactual history, speculation about how things might have become, if things had happened differently is regarded unprofessional by most historians. Yet to reflect on a past that might have been need not be a fool's errand; in such instances disappointment may rekindle hope. The Kennedy era seems ripe for such reflection. For the record: John F. Kennedy was inaugurated president of the United

States on January 20, 1961 and served until his death by assassination on November 22, 1963. He was succeeded by Lyndon Johnson, the Vice President, who was re-elected in his own right in 1964. Johnson left office on January 20, 1969, and was succeeded by Richard Nixon.

So, I will ask, what if John Kennedy had lived to complete his presidency in the normal course of eight years. In 1960, the Kennedy-Johnson ticket must have seemed ideal to accomplish the goals that Kennedy laid out in his speech. In retrospect. Its ending was tragic. Kennedy's presidency was ended by an assassin's bullet; and Johnson led the nation into war. But what if Kennedy had lived. He was a political realist. And his realism enabled him to see the folly of armed ideological struggle. The fiasco at the Bay of Pigs in April 1961 taught him this lesson. He took the blame for it and resolved never to make the same mistake again. Nine months later Kennedy became engaged in a conflict of wills with Nikita Khrushchev regarding the Soviet installation of missiles in Cuba; it became a war of words that Kennedy won and his victory prevented a catastrophic world conflict. It is also likely that Kennedy would have early disengaged in Vietnam. The Peace Corps is also part of Kennedy's legacy; its purpose was "to promote world peace and friendship". Had he lived, the Cold War might have ended sooner.

So much for JFK; and what of LBJ? That we remember them by their initials suggests that both saw themselves as heirs of FDR. Where Kennedy excelled in international politics, Johnson was a master of domestic affairs and practical politics. The Civil Rights legislation enacted during his presidency was already in the works before he became president; Johnson was the chief designer and mover of it. Domestically, he was to the left of Kennedy. And had Kennedy lived and served out his terms, it is likely that Johnson would have succeeded him, and the Great Society might have become a reality and not just a dream. And the nation might have been spared the Nixon years.

But none of this happened. Back to reality, JFK was assassinated, and LBJ led this nation into a war that it subsequently lost. Martin Luther King was murdered in April 1968, and two months later, Robert F. Kennedy suffered the same fate, just after he won the Democratic primary in California. Richard Nixon was elected President in 1968, and reelected in 1972, which brought us Watergate. Nixon's crooked heir, Donald J. Trump was elected President of the United States in 2016. Twice impeached, and then defeated in a bid for reelection. He waits in the wings, threatening a return. And the American political comedy plays on

Postscript: The historian Robert Dallek, who is also a Kennedy biographer *(An Unfinished Life: John F. Kennedy, 1917–1963)*, has expressed puzzlement that many regard JFK as one of the nation's greatest presidents, a judgment that cannot be based on facts, for there are so few of them. He attributes it to the myth that has grown around Kennedy since his death, a product of wishful thinking and romance infused with sex and glamour. Dallek believes that the attribution is undeserved, that the walls of Camelot were made of cardboard. Yet the New Frontier is still there, waiting for a great person to lead the nation across it.

What Does It All Mean?

THIS IS THE FINAL ESSAY IN MY SERIES about the American Political Tradition. The time has come for closing comments, a summation telling what it all means. But now that I have reached this point, I am lost for words. I have written too much to be able to summarize it all in a few sentences, or even a few dozen of them, and as I review what I have written, I become painfully aware that much has been left out. There is no essay about Jane Addams (1860–1935) or Martin Luther King (1929-68) or James Baldwin (1924–87); and there are many more, more than enough for another series.

But I must finish what I started and end this series with a closing statement.

The meaning of America may be summed up by the concluding phrase from the pledge of allegiance: "one nation indivisible, with liberty and justice for all".

The United States of America is a union of States that were once independent and sovereign; a civil war was fought over the question whether any state or group of them had the right to secede from the union. The Secessionists were defeated, and the Union was preserved, and the nation became irrevocably one.

Even so, the Confederacy is a shameful memory, a stain on the fabric of American history. For what motivated the secessionist states to secede was an ignoble desire to preserve the institution of slavery. Their defeat brought an end to slavery in the United States; all slaves were set free and made citizens with all the rights and privileges appertaining thereto. Many former slaves fought and died to preserve the Union, and they proved their heroism and nobility. Even more, Black genius has made an indelible mark on American culture, to which Black experience has added richness and depth.

The meaning of the political traditions of this nation may also be summed up by the preamble of the Constitution, which is worth quoting—Indeed, we should all know it by heart and recite it every morning when we awake as a reminder of our true identity.

> "We the people of the United States,
> in order to form a more perfect Union,
> establish Justice, insure domestic
> Tranquility, provide for the common
> Defense, promote the general Welfare, and
> secure the Blessings of Liberty to ourselves

and to our Posterity, do ordain and
establish this Constitution for the United
States of America."

The United States is a union of states that exists under the rule of law, and the purposes of this law are summed up in these great words: *Union, Justice, domestic Tranquility, common Defense, general Welfare, the Blessings of Liberty for all the people now and forever.*

But justice and the blessings of liberty have not been universally bestowed, which adds another unfinished chapter to the narrative that I tried to spell out over the past year. The United States of America is a product of the European colonization of the Western hemisphere that began after the voyages of Columbus. The European colonizers who settled here did not believe in human equality. They came to get rich. And, to that end, they committed many egregious wrongs, which today would be judged to be crimes against humanity. The first, beginning with Columbus, was the enslavement and genocide of indigenous people; another was the African slave trade and the American institution of slavery, which made some Americans very rich indeed, among them two of our most eminent founders, who are enshrined at Mount Rushmore. The enduring legacy of these wrongs is racism; it has taken root in the minds of the descendants of the colonizers, and other white folk who came after them, and it has remained like a malignancy doing its dreadful work in the body politic down to the present day. The racially motivated murders of African Americans by White police officers are among its consequences. And such crimes are likely to continue as long as the hateful evil of racism persists, as it does even in Middlebury.

The United States aspires to be a great nation, but the principal source of its greatness resides in its founding principles of freedom and equality, and not until those principles are fully established and universally realized will it ever become great. Like a divine injunction, Americans must write the words "freedom and equality" on the doorposts of their houses and inscribe them in their hearts and join the struggle to achieve them until they become a reality throughout all of the land.

This was the dream of Martin Luther King. And his dream captures what this nation means. So, I conclude this series with his prophetic words.

> "I have a dream that one day this nation will rise up and live out the true meaning of its creed 'we hold these truths to be self evident, that all men are created equal' …
>
> "I have a dream that one day on the red hills of Georgia, the sons of former slaves and sons of former slave owners will be able to sit down together at the table of brotherhood.…

"I have a dream that my four little children will one day live in a nation where they will not be judged by the color of their skin but by the content of their character.

"I have a dream that one day down in Alabama, with its vicious racists, … one day right there in Alabama little black boys and black girls will be able to join hands with little white boys and white girls as sisters and brothers.….

"This is the faith that I go back to the South with. With this faith we will be able to hew out of the mountain of despair a figure of hope. **With this faith we will be able to transform the jangling discords of our nation into a beautiful symphony of brotherhood.**"

And one very last word from the goodly fellowship of the prophets: "Let justice roll down like waters, and righteousness like an ever flowing stream" (Amos 5:24), from which it follows as surely as the night follows the day that BLACK LIVES MATTER.

About the Author

Victor Nuovo was born and raised in New York City. As a graduate student he attended Union Theological Seminary and Columbia University, receiving his Ph.D. from Columbia in 1964. In 1962 Victor joined the faculty of Middlebury College, Middlebury, Vermont, and first taught religion and then philosophy, becoming chair of the department. He retired from Middlebury in 1994 as Charles A. Dana Professor of Philosophy Emeritus. In 1996 he was appointed Visiting Fellow at Harris Manchester College, Oxford, and reappointed the following year as a Senior Research Fellow, a position he still holds.

Victor's area of specialty is the history of philosophy, in particular, 17th century English philosophy. He has published six books about the English philosopher John Locke, most recently, *John Locke: The Philosopher as Christian Virtuoso* (Oxford University Press). In 2006 he was elected to the Town of Middlebury's select board and served on the board for more than ten years.

Victor has been married since 1953 to Betty Nuovo, a former Vermont State Representative. They have two sons and four grandchildren and reside in Middlebury, Vermont.

www.ingramcontent.com/pod-product-compliance
Lightning Source LLC
Chambersburg PA
CBHW021438070526
44577CB00002B/208